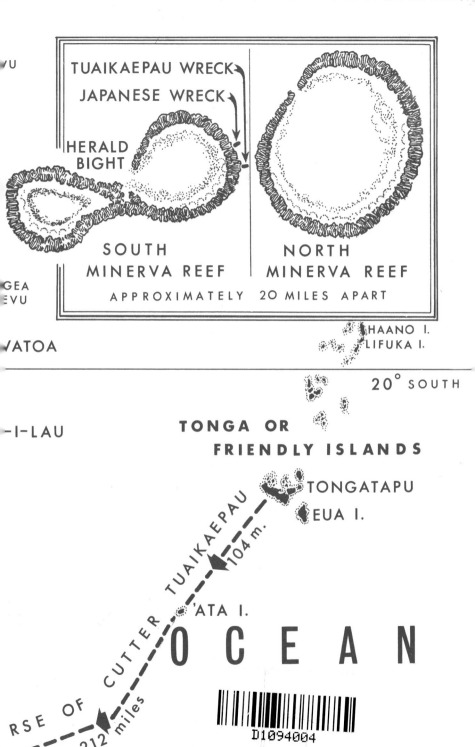

TUAIKAEPAU WRECK
JAPANESE WRECK

HERALD
BIGHT

SOUTH
MINERVA REEF

NORTH
MINERVA REEF

APPROXIMATELY 20 MILES APART

VU

GEA
EVU

VATOA

HAANO I.
LIFUKA I.

20° SOUTH

-I-LAU

**TONGA OR
FRIENDLY ISLANDS**

TONGATAPU
EUA I.

COURSE OF CUTTER TUAIKAEPAU

104 m.

'ATA I.

OCEAN

212 miles

MINERVA REEF

Minerva Reef

OLAF RUHEN

Line Drawings by
CLEM SEALE

THE ADVENTURERS CLUB

LONDON

THE ADVENTURERS CLUB

178-202 Great Portland Street, London, W.1

First published by Angus & Robertson Ltd, 1963

This edition 1965

Printed in England by Balding + Mansell Ltd of Wisbech
and bound by Wm. Brendon & Son Ltd of Tiptree.

Acknowledgments

I WOULD be ungrateful if I did not record the very generous and energetic co-operation I had from everyone connected with the *Minerva Reef* story, in particular the survivors themselves, for I am honoured to call them friends.

I am also indebted to His Royal Highness Prince Tungi, K.B.E., Premier of Tonga; to the Government Secretary, Mr R. C. G. Strick; to Mr R. W. Robson, director, and Mr L. G. Usher, editor, of the Fiji Times and Herald Ltd.; to Air Vice-Marshal I. G. Morrison, Chief of Staff of the Royal New Zealand Air Force, together with some of his officers; to Mr R. G. Haggett, manager of Tonga Radio, and his chief announcer, 'Uliti Palu; to Miss Jean Whyte of the Fisher Library at the University of Sydney; to Dr Ralph Huntley, Dr Stephen Mayne and Dr Bruce Low, of Sydney; to Mr Tofa Ramsay and Mr Carl Reichelman of Nuku'alofa, and others. I owe special thanks to Enoki Faletau, Government Interpreter of Tonga, for his co-operation and his patience.

Photographs are by courtesy of the Royal New Zealand Air Force, Squadron Leader Kelvin R. Bremner, the Fiji Times and Herald Ltd., and Mr Stan Whippy of the *Fiji Times*.

OLAF RUHEN

Publishers' Note

THE publishers are indebted to Esther Faigan of Minerva Bookshop Limited, Auckland—publishers of the New Zealand edition of *Minerva Reef*—for her enterprise in flying to Suva when the castaways' story was first made known. This quick action made it possible for them to acquire their rights in the story.

THE CREW

Tevita (David) Fifita, Captain.

Ve'etutu Pahulu, Mate.

Sateki Fifita, deckhand, and David's eldest son.

Talo Fifita, deckhand, and David's illegitimate son.

Tevita (David) Uaisele, ship's carpenter.

Fine Feuiaki, ship's engineer.

Sione (Johnny) Lousi, deckhand.

THE PASSENGERS

Fatai Efiafi, a widower at a loose end.

Vaiangina Unga, a copra planter.

Viliame Fa'onuku, known as *William Fa*, a carpenter.

Teiapa'a Bloomfield, a taxi-driver.

Soakai Pulu, retired heavyweight boxing champion of Tonga.

Fetaiaki Pulu, Soakai's son, another boxer.

Sione (Johnny) Sikimeti, a young boxer under Soakai's management.

Sipa Fine, current heavyweight and light-heavy boxing champion of Tonga.

Finau Laione, Sipa's cousin, a young boxer.

Saia Peni, a self-trained boxer.

Chapter One

THE reef, not yet an atoll, more than a shoal, has thrust its fortress walls towards the light as though with surety and purpose, climbing from the unillumined depths towards the life-giving radiance essential to its architects, the coral polyps. But at the surface of the sea its further growth is inhibited; exposure to air and sun destroys its builders, and storms carve off its higher structures and lay them low. For the reef to become an atoll it must wait the centuries through, until the violence of waters has thrown an accumulation of coral masses from its flanks upon its surface, until the great lagoon that forms its centre has silted up in such an area that it will trap the driftwood and detritus that sails that way: the discarded husks of coconuts, and the flotsam of faraway harbours. There is, additionally, the chance that some great earth movement will one day thrust it bodily in air, and the reef is situated in a place subject to just such movements.

Until some such time it lies beneath the surface of the

full-tide ocean, a fathom down, with the ebb exposing, for an hour each day, a section of its circumference that varies between a hundred and five hundred yards in width. The centre of the surface thus exposed is made of sand and small coral fragments, not in great depth. A foot or two below lies the coral body, a mass of figured carbonate of lime, surprisingly hard, and sharp as a razor as to certain of its edges. The texture of this body stone—for stone it is, despite its animal origin—may be estimated without a closer observation, for, dotted on the surface, are masses of the same coral thrown there by storms that dislodged them from the beetling, overhanging, underwater cliffs that give this sand protection.

Such masses look black at a little distance, throwing no light. Close at hand, they are a uniform steel-grey; so solid and heavy that it seems impossible that any force of water or of air could have conveyed them to these their resting-places. And they are the exceptions. The majority of such dislodged masses rolled down the underwater cliffs to buttress the foundations of the reef a half-mile and more beneath the sea's surface, or to be trapped in some embrasure of its steep and formidable walls.

On the lagoon side of this sand, where on calm and windless days the water lies as still and innocent as in a reservoir, the receding tide leaves coral pools, rich with a fantasy of marine life centuries undisturbed. Great fish sun themselves in inadequate enclosures, secure in the knowledge that the rising tide will open the walls of their self-chosen prisons; cowries and spider-shells abandon locomotion until such time as the water shall come again; even the turtles, wariest of all the creatures in this ocean sanctuary, are sometimes to be caught at a disadvantage here. From crevices in all the pools the sea-egg's porcupine armour thrusts into sight; the feelers of crayfish wave aimlessly; glimpses of patterned skin betray the dogfish

2

and the eel where they have sought the protection of the rocks. Less tasty morsels, the bêche-de-mer and the star-fish, sprawl across the open centres of the pools; corals and their cousins the anemones are brilliant in colours and combinations of colours for which even the liveliest im-aginations are unprepared. Hermit crabs battle for posses-sion of shells recently discarded; small fish put themselves in hazard of the stinging weeds.

On the ocean side the submarine scenery is more com-plex still. You come to it across an area where surging waves spend out what energy is left to them after their negotiation of the outer ramparts, and ripple on ineffect-ively across the interior sand. At high water, in times of storm, the armies of waves sweep by triumphantly. Noth-ing then stands in their road. But only on the most peace-ful of days has man looked over the seaward edge of the South Minerva Reef; only a particular kind of man, and then in clement weather.

The reef is one of the most isolated in the central part of the Pacific Ocean; it lies in temperate regions but near the Tropic of Capricorn. A line drawn north-eastward, connecting it with the main island of the tropical Tonga group, is the baseline of a triangle, nearly isosceles, of which the apex is the main island of the Fiji group, 380 miles north-west of Minerva. Its distance from Tonga is only 260 miles, but it lies in such a direction that it is not approached by even the most minor of shipping lines. Few people have seen the reef, and those only briefly.

Its seaward verge is a steep and fearsome construction of pinnacle and abyss, water-hidden. The tortuosity of this construction is brought to excess upon the eastern and southern shores of the reef, because it lies within the range of the trade winds in the south-eastern monsoon; and it is from this direction and from just west of south that the worst of the seas here, and the most consistent, are generated.

Here on this outer verge the marine life is more abundant than ever. The soundings taken just beyond the reef show depths of 300 and 450 fathoms, or no bottom at over 200. This suits the sharks, which by some advantage of their metabolism can cruise along the underwater precipice and prey on travelling fish, slowed down, or dizzied perhaps, by the swift changes of pressure. And there are sharks here in great abundance; and fish for them to prey on. The smaller predators that feed the shark are themselves fed to repletion upon still lesser victims.

Here the corals and anemones are magnificent; here is a variety of animals, not all of them as yet in human knowledge.

In days of storm the place is a fury; the waves come in from the south-east driven by a wind no land has diverted; when the south-wester sweeps up all the way from the Antarctic to displace the Trades—as here, outside the limits of the Tropics, it frequently does—it comes without obstruction over the whole width of the Tasman Sea.

The coral rock, like coral everywhere, is tunnelled and holed and riven; the advancing seas, smashing against the underwater cliffs, find apertures and blowholes, and at low tide they pour their energies into such a fantasy of spouting water that the observing eye is hypnotized; no fountain architect ever envisaged such a wild ambitious pattern; none ever commanded the power essential for its creation.

Far eastward of the reef the ocean floor is cleft by a valley that could swallow the Himalayas and leave them sunk a mile beneath the ocean surface. This is the Tonga Deep where in 1957 the Russian ship *Vityaz* made a sounding of 35,567 feet, and where, in time to come, still other ships, with instruments we have not yet created, will probe

4

the mysteries of a world, perhaps based even deeper, of which we have no knowledge.

This cleft, with its Pacific fellows the Mariana Trench, the Challenger Depth, the Japan Trench, we know to be associated with the gravity anomalies that help us shape the geoid, and with vulcanism, and high seismic activity. From its edge the land running back to the west lies at a great depth too; it is criss-crossed with submarine valleys and knobbed with hills, but picks up height in a more or less regular fashion. Approximately in latitude 23 degrees south, longitude 179 west, a submarine plateau is centred. This plateau, split from east to west by a lesser valley a mile deep, is about twenty-eight miles long and runs north-north-east and south-south-west. Its depth is between 300 and 600 fathoms, and from each of its two related components there rises the massive coral base of a reef.

South Minerva is itself a welding of two atolls, each of which, standing alone, would form a rough circle approximately seven and a half miles in circumference. The axis on which they lie runs east-north-east from the most westerly point; and on this axis they form a figure-of-eight, bent slightly upwards, towards the Equator. In nautical works they are referred to as the western lagoon and the northern one. A confusion of coral practically separates them at low water, but there are narrow and shallow connecting channels which small boats could negotiate.

At the junction, however, and leading back from the open sea in the bay to the north into the northern lagoon there is a good channel four or five hundred yards wide, with bottom at thirteen fathoms; a channel any ship could negotiate. Certainly there are isolated rocks, niggerheads of coral, that come within a couple of fathoms of the surface, but they are all so prominent as to be readily observable from a masthead.

Within the northern lagoon, once this entrance is cleared,

5

there is perfectly clear and deep water; but the knolls of coral that border the shores of both lagoons make it difficult to operate even small dinghies. At high water small boats can cross from one lagoon to the other over the tops of the formations.

The sea breaks heavily on the southernmost side of the junction of the two atolls, which from their shape entrap and increase the regular south-east swell; and a further contribution to the heaviness of the surf here comes from the set; the general current which in this part of the Pacific may run as strongly as two knots towards the west. The solid portion of the reef is highest here because of this circumstance; it has been built up by a notable collection of coral blocks riven from the deep. Here, too, the sandbar within is wider; here, in the normal course of events, in a thousand years or two an island will be formed; and, being formed, will catch here the greatest share of sea-wrack.

On the northern side of the junction of the two atolls the sandbar is wide, but lower. There is a good anchorage here in the south-west season; about 500 yards from the edge of the outer reef is good ground in depths of from ten to twenty fathoms.

Eighteen miles to the north-east is the related shoal or reef of North Minerva; as old, no older, and in the same cycle of formation; a simple reef by reason of the fact that it forms but a single atoll at low water. The lagoon, except at the edges of the reef, is sandy and clear of coral; the light, bright blue it reflects in sunlight testifies to this to trained aerial observers. It is eleven miles in circumference, and thus is a little smaller than South Minerva, which is fourteen miles around. Over the period that North Minerva has come under the notice of mariners it has shoaled a fathom or two. The reef has an entrance on the north-west side, not more than 300 yards wide, but holding a depth of thirteen fathoms, and uncomplicated by individual rocks. Even on the sheltered side of the reef, however, there is no anchorage, for the depths are too great.

The ground from which these undersea mountains spring now offers no evidence as to the way in which they had their birth, unless the occasional presence of volcanic cinders brought up by the log is significant. But it need not be: the Tonga group, where volcanoes are plentiful, is only 260 miles away; and, moreover, in this part of ocean old Vulcan often fires his forge beneath the waves.

Something of this problem must have concerned Captain H. M. Denham, R.N., F.R.S., when, in H.M.S. *Herald*, in 1854, he surveyed and named these two reefs. "I obtained soundings," he wrote, "and brought up the bottom at nine hundred and sixty seven fathoms, about midway between them. The greater part of this sounding consists of the shells of many microscopic species of *Foraminifera*. It also contains several specimens of a *styliola*, abundantly taken everywhere in the Pacific in the towing net. Mixed up with the sand there are a few fragments of dead slender *cellepora*, a piece of a *bulla*, and several minute detached crystals of smoky quartz, prismatic, and terminated by five-sided pyramids."

Prior to Denham's survey the charts, for nearly thirty years, had contained the indication of a huge area of intersecting reefs, named Nicholson's shoals. As shown, they covered an area of twenty miles by more than a hundred, and their reduction to the two reefs opened a great swathe of ocean to mariners. Commander C. F. Oldham, in H.M.S. *Egeria*, added to knowledge of the reefs in 1889. But not much sea traffic was likely to encounter them.

They lay far away from any sea routes; the direct course between Tonga and New Zealand lay far to the east, between Tonga and Sydney to the north, between Fiji and New Zealand to the west. The busy traffic between Pacific islands moved all to the northward. Not even the air routes go anywhere near this part of ocean. The trade winds here are not dependable. They frequently come from the east rather than the south-east, and are more readily displaced here by a variety of other winds, being at the southern end of their influence. The reefs are affected by the variations of the cyclone seasons.

So while they offer a considerable menace to such men as may be in their vicinity, there are few reasons or occasions to take men there; and only men who, of their nature, probe and penetrate the unknown places—the adventurers, the investigators—come within the orbit of that menace. They are of the breed of men who become the racial heroes; they stand out among the crowd for one distinguishing characteristic, and that is physical courage.

In the early days of European penetration of the South Pacific the seas below Tonga were lively with pods of whales; the New Zealand path of whale migration to the Antarctic lies principally to the west of Fiji; but there was good hunting in Tongan waters too, and it was to these islands that the whalers primarily looked for human company; for most of them feared the cannibals of Fiji.

Captain Denham named the reefs for the whaler *Minerva*, which sailed from Sydney in New South Wales on 16th August 1829 to capture whales in Tongan waters. She had a complement of twenty-three men and a dog. She was victualled for a year, and prepared to sail all the waters between Tonga and the Solomons in search of her quarry. Her sailing-master, Peter Bays, very properly made her easting first, and she sighted the Three Kings Island in the North of New Zealand after fifteen days; a voyage longer than the weather warranted, for she sprung some of her head timbers after five days on the violent Tasman Sea, and thereafter kept hands at the pumps continually.

The forecastle was awash, and the crew, in wet beds, with wet gear, were truly miserable.

But on 1st September they picked up a strong south-wester, and raced before it to the Tropics. It veered to south, and then south-east, so that they kept a heading rather more westerly than they had planned. They saw no whales, but on the seventh day out of New Zealand they harpooned a porpoise from the bows and tried out its blubber for their first oil.

In this year Pacific charts showed Nicholson's shoals, but only earlier editions were available in Sydney at the time of *Minerva's* departure. Peter Bays claimed familiarity with Tongan and Fijian waters; but he was confident that they sailed in safety when, at 2 a.m. on 9th September, the brig struck hard upon what is now recognized as South Minerva.

Her bow drove high upon the reef on the south-eastern shore. The tide was then towards its peak, and this fact saved them all, some for a later disaster. A whaler's boats were ever ready at the davits, and her men were skilled boatmen. The captain's boat was launched first, but a steep sea clutched it before they were ready to row, and ripped tackle and davit from the *Minerva's* side; though in the confusion they did not know, but thought they had run free. They got the oars out and attempted to clear southward, into the wind and away from the reef ahead, but a second sea lifted them up, and on its peak, either by magnificent seamanship or from some subconscious urge towards self-preservation, they backed water and rode it over the dangerous rocks into the lagoon.

When they saw that they were still towing the tackle and davit, when they realized that they had cleared the snags of the coral beneath the surface, they attributed their preservation to God; for if this unwieldy drogue had fouled a group of niggerheads and there held tight, their

9

frail boat, of half-inch planking worked down to a third or less, would have splintered to fragments, and every soul of them must have perished.

Garrett the mate was in the boat with the captain; in half an hour they heard a shout and responded, and were joined by the second mate, Shean, with his crew. He brought the news that Lewis, the whaling-master (and properly, in these circumstances, the master of the expedition), was drunk; he was "raving about the decks like one distracted and would not leave" though heavy seas were sweeping the *Minerva* from stern to stem.

Not long afterwards they saw a light aboard *Minerva*, and then a considerable time elapsed; at last Lewis's boat hove in sight, but without Lewis, who, with two drunken companions (his boat-crew reported), would not leave the wrecked brig.

Before daylight came some pieces of the wreck passed them; as well as casks for oil, sea-chests, and pieces of salt pork. With the light the reef was uncovered; the tide had fallen, and they unloaded the smallest boat and reduced its crew to four, which four presently approached the remains of the *Minerva* and rescued the three men and the dog from a dubious shelter in the forepart.

After the night's battering this was the only part remaining; the men upon the wreck had cut away the spare boat and then the masts, in order to reduce resistance to the seas; and then had taken shelter between the weather bulwarks and an installation of copper boilers for trying down blubber; but in the night the brig parted abaft the mainmast, and they had just time to run and secure themselves to the bowsprit.

They had solaced themselves in this extremity with yet more liquor which they had carried with them, and were still dead drunk; determined not to leave but to stay and build a storm-house upon the wreck, and then a boat large enough to take them all. It was noon before they were carried, helpless with liquor, to the boats; and there were subdued, at some risk to their rescuers.

Meantime the other two boats had been collecting casks of water and provisions, these fortunately being abundant and close at hand. When, in some trepidation and with great difficulty, they had cleared the reef again for the open sea the twenty-three men were distributed amongst three boats, reasonably well found, but heavily laden for such seas as those in which they lay. They attached wash-cloths to the gunwales to reduce the intake of sea-water; but the boat which Bays, the sailing-master, commanded had been partly stove and was leaking badly.

Consequently they were obliged to reef down her sails, and dropped so far behind that the others bore down to speak them. They were in no mind to lose their company upon the wild ocean, and so reefed out, and kept up for a while; but the wind freshened more, and again they reefed and fell behind. They had no choice, because of the quantities of water entering the boat. Again the others bore down, but after speaking them Shean, the second mate, became impatient, and headed for Tonga, far to the north and east.

Lewis, the whaling-master, was more considerate. When the case for Bays and his men was shown to be desperate he hove to, and in some degree kept the weather from the stricken boat throughout the night.

In this he saved his life. For Shean, driving on, must have struck the North Minerva; no trace of him or his crew was ever seen again. The other two boats saw the reef in the night; they could not identify it, but they reported drifting past foul ground, and there was none other in those waters.

On the following day they killed two large sharks with the whaling spades they carried; and a little later Bays's boat was in such straits that they got the carpenter over

B

from Lewis's boat to make and supervise repairs. Under his instructions they frapped the planks together with a binding of new canvas; the expected shrinkage made a tighter boat of it; but the frapping reduced their speed so much, and Lewis drew so far ahead that they cut it away and, since they carried superior sail, caught up with him; and there, against a sullen opposition, they transferred to Lewis's boat, which now carried fifteen men, a dog, and provisions; but in the transfer they left their fresh water behind.

When they took stock they found they had two biscuits, two pounds of pork, and two pounds of cheese a man; but all of it was sodden with sea-water. They also had seven gallons of drinking-water in two stinking oil-kegs, wherein globules of rancid whale-oil floated still. They threw overboard their muskets, harpoons, lances, and extra clothing; but they were low in the water: when all was level one plank, or rather less than six inches, was all their freeboard. They had a heavy sea, and a wind so fresh that for three hours they rafted the boat, just letting it drift before the wind.

They still had rum; Lewis apparently had seen to that; and it served to make the water drinkable. The rum ran out on 13th September; and the water ration was reduced to three sips a man a day, the "sips" being measured out with the lid of a tinder-box.

On the fourteenth they were drinking sea-water and their own urine; and thirst became unbearable. Bays, the captain, was so intent upon relieving his thirst that his companions refused him the bailer. They chewed lead to produce a saliva; two pieces alternately, changing them over as the metal in the air became cold. Between one such resource or another they suffered from "a bloody and white flux"; and their buttocks were blistered and bleeding from

12

the soaked condition of their clothes, and from holding their positions in the boat.

On 15th September they had their last three sips of water. Towards noon they were preparing to slaughter the dog, when they sighted land. They staved in their whaleboat on the encircling reef, but came ashore safely, and slaked their thirst with coconuts, which were numerous.

They thought the island to be uninhabited; but on the following day they were quite suddenly surrounded by "savages". Instead of being killed, as they feared, they were treated kindly, and taken to the chief of the island who, because of illness, was permanently confined to his hut, and who ordered that all their possessions be given back to them, and that help might be given them to fix their boat. It was the island of Vatoa, one of the Outer Lau group between Fiji and Tonga, and inhabited by Tongans.

In their subsequent adventures eight of the *Minerva* men remained upon the island while the other seven set out in the repaired boat, to wreck it again, and again to be succoured by Tongans on an island before they returned by way of New Zealand to Sydney. The tribulations of the *Minerva* men are almost forgotten now; but they have put a name on the charts that remains.

No one will ever complete the tally of wrecks for which the reefs have been responsible; it would probably include some of the great double canoes of Fiji, vessels larger, faster, and more efficient into the wind than any of the European vessels of discovery that encountered them, and carrying more numerous crews.

The lesser vessels of Tonga must have known the reefs; they were commanded by seamen no less efficient than the Fijians, and were smaller only because of the limited supplies of suitable Tongan timbers.

Since the European has invaded the Pacific the list of

wrecks, expanding with the years, has included vessels named and identified; but, European or islander, few castaways have survived to tell their tales. While it is true that the reefs show out by reason of their breakers, while it is true that the atypical thunder of such seas is audible at considerable distances, there are times of storm when sight and sound of the reef are lost in the general maelstrom of vibration and darkness; and many and many a mystery of the ocean would be solved if the Minervas uncovered all their secrets.

It is in storm that the reef is dangerous; in storm and driving seas; and particularly for small windships. The limitations of these ships sometimes take them far from accustomed sea-routes, and most of them that have encountered the reef have been lost; in a very few instances a wreck has survived long enough to afford a temporary shelter and an eventual salvation to its complement.

The *Strathcona*, a schooner built in Auckland, New Zealand, at the beginning of the 1914-18 war, defied the superstition of the sea by sailing on her maiden voyage on a Friday, with a total complement of thirteen. She was built by Charles Bailey, whose yard has turned out many a vessel that subsequently became the pride of some island port; and the materials he used would be hard to duplicate today: ribs of sawn New Zealand ironwood, and planking of kauri heartwood.

She was owned by the Pacific Cable Board, and her mission was to provision the cable station at Fanning Island, north of the Equator. Six days out from Auckland, pointing up on a starboard tack, she hit hard upon South Minerva, towards the top of the tide, when the commotion of waters was least observable. She drove up high, right out of the water, traversing the outer coral bank and coming to rest upon the sand, with her bottom torn out of her and her back broken.

14

The crew stayed with the ship, and next morning at low water they lowered the undamaged boats, the launch and the whale-boat, onto the reef and loaded them with food. As the tide rose they were floated into the lagoon.

The *Strathcona* was by no means immovable as she lay; therefore the crew took shelter in the boats at every rising tide; Captain W. Robertson and the second mate with six others occupying the 22-foot launch, and the mate and four others in the 16-foot whale-boat. Thus they spent several days.

As soon as they assessed their position they began to build a raft from the *Strathcona's* masts and gaffs, and such planking as they could salvage. They had no use for this raft in navigation; its purpose was simply to give them a sleeping-place above the waves, and to release one of the boats so that it could go for help. They added to it as they could, and moored it to the reef itself with wire hawsers. During periods of bad weather the men on the raft were up to their waists in the seas which swept over them; but they erected narrow sleeping-platforms which, on most nights, offered them security.

Sixteen days after the wreck Captain Robertson, accompanied by the cook and two able seamen, set off for the nearest land, the coral-girt island of Ono-i-Lau to the north. Here he enlisted the aid of a native-owned cutter, and came back to rescue his fellows.

In the meantime, however, the *Strathcona* had been posted missing; and the Pacific Cable Board sent its ship *Iris* in search; though it had no way of knowing that the *Strathcona* had not been lost to enemy action. The Board must have suspected the Minervas, for the *Iris* found the survivors on their raft twenty-five days after the wreck. She also encountered the Ono-i-Lau cutter, from which Captain Robertson and his companions were transhipped. Most of the men were in a bad way; they were unused to coral, and the cuts and slashes they had sustained were poisoned; but all of them survived.

There were other wrecks on the Minervas, and from some of them were other survivors; but there were many that remained mysteries. In 1917 there was a wrecked hull clearly visible on North Minerva; the years and the seas destroyed it; but where it lay some evidence will remain; certainly the anchors, for anchors are the headstones of dead and vanished ships.

In 1960 a Japanese fishing vessel was wrecked on the eastern end of South Minerva. She was one of half a dozen vessels of the same sort wrecked and abandoned on reefs near Fiji; and, though nothing much is known of her, there could have been no human tragedy associated with her end. She was abandoned in perfect order; her efficient radio transmitter—an MF/DF set with which at normal times she kept touch with her mother ship, sometimes at ranges exceeding a thousand miles—was unharmed. Her crew left with their possessions, in good order; the tools were taken from the engine-room, the cutlery and crockery from the galley. Her fishing-gear stayed with her, but otherwise the evidence that remained with the wreck testified to orderly withdrawal.

And then, on the night of 7th July 1962, the cutter *Tuaikaepau*, cracking along at seven knots under sail, on a port tack, pointing up hard into the wind, ran upon the reef, and under the battering of a merciless sea was reduced to a wrack of floating planks within a few hours, so that the seventeen men who formed the crew found themselves, in the hours of darkness, without a ship, without a small boat, upon a reef which within hours, they knew, would be deep beneath the tide. Their condition was as hopeless as any that has faced the luckless mariners of history. They had nothing but their faith; and some of them were unacquainted with the sea.

16

But their faith was strong. They were Tongans, a people as resourceful as any in the world; a people noted for delivering of their best under stress. They survived, or a majority of them survived. They kept themselves alive for a hundred and two days upon that reef; and they did more. For they encompassed their own rescue; and to do so they built their own craft, using an unbelievably poor handful of inadequate tools to produce a small decked vessel of which a boat-builder could have been proud.

Faith and loyalty armoured them; they worked to a common end until work became impossible. And though some of them weakened and broke the communal rules they devised; though there were dissensions and quarrels; though some were no better than the average of us all, they had a magnificent integrity which brought them at last to the triumph of safety. This is their story, and the story of Tevita (David) Fifita, the great-hearted man who brought them home at last.

It is primarily a story laced with tragedy. But even the sacrifices were triumphant, for lives were given voluntarily for the common weal, in circumstances that will be regarded as epic, down the generations. It is a story that shouts a glory of Tonga; but more than that, it hymns the transcendent potential of the human kind; it testifies to the ability of man to endure for long periods and, enduring, to work, to build, to have faith, and to keep the confidence to worship God and to lean upon the future.

Only heroes can subsist through such great pressures as Minerva Reef can invoke. These were heroes, and they lived such a legend here as cannot be forgotten.

Chapter Two

PERHAPS it was fitting for the *Tuaikaepau* to end her sailing days upon the savage teeth of Minerva; it was not her fate to rot away in a tropical harbour, to die by inches of neglect or age; no seaman ever sorrowed to see that beautiful hull converted to base or inferior purposes in sheltered waters. She was a beautiful ship and remained beautiful to her last day. Perhaps, indeed, she never looked better than in that last moment before the flint-edged stone ripped into her bottom; she was on her best course and giving of her best performance.

She had a long career. She was launched in 1902 from that same Bailey yard in Auckland as launched the *Strathcona*; but her life was sixty years; the *Strathcona's* was six days. The owners who first commissioned her were Captain Stanhope and a Mr Shakespear, of Great Barrier Island. She was a keeler, 51 feet overall; and, conceived in a year of transition, she had features that wedded the beauty of the past to the innovations of the century.

Thus she still retained the old-fashioned clipper bow (which, in fact, was a feature of the early Bailey yachts), but had the fuller midship section modern in the years of her birth, and a tiny tuck stern with a very long overhang.

Captain Stanhope soon acquired his partner's interest in the yacht, then named *Ilex*; and took her to Stewart Island, south of the South Island of New Zealand, where she proved her worth in the rough weather of the Roaring Forties. Her next owner, Mr J. Macky, took her back to Auckland, where he raced her successfully on the Waitemata Harbour. At a later stage still, and under still another owner, she was converted to yawl rig for easier handling; and as a yawl she cruised extensively round the New Zealand coast. Her then owner, Mr E. H. Northcroft, later Mr Justice Northcroft, entertained the Governor-General of New Zealand, Lord Bledisloe, aboard her; and so she continued, one of the aristocrats of the New Zealand fleet.

Mr N. W. Thomas circumnavigated New Zealand in her in 1946; a year and a voyage in which she nearly came to her end. The storms of the south-west coast drove her into Bligh Sound, a deep drowned valley in a chain of valleys which much resemble, if indeed they do not surpass, the fjords of Norway. In the sound the gale was funnelled between the next-to-perpendicular walls, and drove the yacht under bare poles right to the end of the seaway. Only the last attempt to anchor was successful; the *Ilex* rounded up to hold fast with all her anchors down in a shallowing bay beyond which lay disaster. Bligh Sound, unlike some of the others on that coast, has an evil reputation for wind; the ground on which the *Ilex* held is the only charted anchorage within its waters.

The same owner sailed *Ilex* across the Tasman to compete unsuccessfully in the Sydney-Hobart ocean race in Australia. She returned safely to Wellington, New Zealand, after seven weeks and voyages totalling 4,000 miles, having added considerably to her reputation for staunchness. The following year Thomas sold her for £6,000 to the Free Church of Tonga.

Tonga-tapu, Sacred Tonga, the Kingdom of the Sacred South, is the last remaining Polynesian self-governing State. By a treaty of friendship signed in 1900 it is under the protection of Great Britain. Its area of 269 square miles, divided among 158 islands, is scattered over 20,000 square miles of ocean lying between latitudes 18 and 23 south, and between 173 and 176 west longitudes; but only thirty-six of these islands carry its population of about 65,000 people, a population rapidly growing.

The islands fall into three distinct groups, Tonga-tapu in the south, Ha'apai in the centre, and Vava'u in the north. Two hundred and ten miles north-west of Vava'u, however, Tin Can Island (Niuafo'ou) is included in the group. Not included are the islands of the Lau group, associated with Fiji, and some of these islands have a population predominantly Tongan.

An exact count of the islands is complicated by the phenomenon of Vulcan, between Tonga-tapu and Ha'apai; a disappearing island which sometimes rises to a height of 400 feet above sea-level, sometimes sinks below the waves, and sometimes is represented by a weird phenomenon of fire upon the surface of the sea.

The island of Tonga-tapu itself is nearly a hundred square miles in extent; more than a third of the entire kingdom. It is completely flat, covered for the most part with coconut plantations and gardens producing taro and bananas. Nuku'alofa is the capital; and on its shorefront the most prominent buildings are the palace of the Queen, Salote, and her chapel.

Most of the islands of Ha'apai too are flat, comprising the rims of coral atolls; and some of them are so nearly at the level of the sea that one marvels at their continued existence. But Vava'u is mountainous; at its centre is a land-locked harbour that has been described as the best in the Pacific, a harbour seven miles long.

While the group lies within the boundary of the Tropics, its climate is best described as semi-tropical; the average mean temperature ranges between 70 and 78 degrees. The absolute maximum rarely reaches 90 degrees or falls below 70; the absolute minimum seldom falls as low as 50 or rises above 70. There are few places in the world where temperatures are so suited to human preferences. And the rainfall is moderate, though a good deal of it comes in heavy convectional falls in the summer months of January, February, and March. The average for the main island is fairly steady at 65 inches annually.

Tongans, like other Polynesians, are happy, easy-going, intelligent, fond of the simple pleasures of dancing and singing. They are good gardeners and intrepid seamen; physically they are well built, and a natural dignity, not unallied to a national aversion to haste, enhances this impression. Dark straight hair, dark eyes, and a light cinnamon skin are no bar to beauty as conceived by Europeans; a tradition of body care with oils of coconut and candlenut, a love of cleanliness, and a close acquaintance with ocean increase the Tongan attraction.

But there are characteristics which set the Tongan apart from other branches of his race; characteristics evolved in the long, and mainly peaceful, occupation of the islands. An intense loyalty to his chiefs has developed into an adherence no less positive to the Queen and the Tongan flag; love of country and local pride have been developed with the realization that this country is the only centre of Polynesian independence.

A system by which all land belongs to the Queen, but under which each Tongan, as he reaches the age of sixteen, may be allotted a coconut plantation of more than eight acres, containing a minimum of 200 palms as well as adequate garden land, has developed a less feckless way of life than you will encounter elsewhere in Polynesia. The Tongan looks ahead, and plans his garden and his storage facilities to give him adequate sustenance throughout the year.

Moreover, he is a more direct man; it was long ago remarked that the Tongan, more than any other native of the Pacific, preferred when fighting to make a frontal attack; he advanced upon fortified places with a show of strength, and some of his battle tactics were tactics of psychological warfare that in Europe were not employed until the 1939-45 conflict.

European schoolteachers in Tonga have shaken their heads over the lack of initiative displayed by their charges; but even the most cynical of them are amazed at the resourcefulness the Tongan calls up when he is placed under stress; he becomes a master of the art of improvisation. His courage is second to none, and he maintains his spirits at a high level, no matter how dark his immediate prospects may seem.

In Tonga, too, as in nowhere else in the Pacific, and in few places throughout the world, women have always been privileged. Traditionally the men did the heavy work of the gardens and the ships; the women engaged in the light task of making the bark cloth they call tapa, and in the weaving of mats. Grooved tapa hammers, beating incessantly upon the inner bark of the paper mulberry, are heard everywhere in Tonga. They are an accompaniment always to laughter and song, for these are happy islands.

Women traditionally have occupied the highest and most sacred positions in the group's social system; Queen Salote, perhaps the last absolute monarch in the world to come by inheritance to her position, was not the first woman to rule her country; and the rights of women have always been preserved on all levels. A woman who, in the past, married a man lower in rank than herself retained the rank proper to her birth; if, however, she married above that station to which she was born she acquired the respect to which her husband was entitled. In the first of these instances she did not elevate her husband to her own rank.

Regardless of station, an additional respect was paid to women merely because of their sex, since they contributed so much to the comfort and happiness of men, and also because they were weaker. It was thought unmanly not to show attention and kind regard to women.

The ancient kingship of Tonga was a sacred one; temporal and spiritual leadership were combined in one person, the Tui Tonga. In the fifteenth century A.D. the incumbent appointed another leader, the Tui Ha'atakalaua, to assume the temporal duties; and it became the custom for the Tui Tonga to marry the daughter of the temporal king. The eldest daughter of such a marriage, the Tui Tonga Fefine, was venerated to such an extent that she could not marry, so high was her rank. Nothing in Tongan morality or custom, however, prevented her from bearing children; if she did, her eldest daughter was called the Tamaha, the "Sacred Child", and was regarded by the Tongans as the most sacred being on earth. Not even her mother, the Tui Tonga Fefine, might eat in her presence.

The last Tamaha, Amelia, died in Ha'apai in 1852; the last Tui Tonga, Laufilitonga by name, died in 1865, and his great granddaughter, Lavinia, married to George II of Tonga, was mother of Queen Salote.

The office of Tui Ha'atakalaua had been in its turn divided centuries before, a younger brother of the incumbent taking over the duties, but not the rewards, of the temporal office, under the title of Tui Kanokupolu. This more vigorous strain persisted; the nineteenth Tui Kanokupolu became George I of Tonga; under the name Taufa'ahau Tupou. But the last Tui Ha'atakalaua to hold office was killed in battle in 1799; from him descended William Tungi, who became the husband of Queen Salote.

Probably the main reason for the high social development of Tongans, and their superb national confidence, is to be found in the many centuries the fortunate islands remained at peace. The first Europeans to find them were the Dutch in the *Eendracht*, on an expedition led by Jacob Le Maire and navigated by Willem Cornelisz Schouten in 1616. They touched at the islands Tafahi, Niuatoputapu, and Niuafo'ou, but then sailed off for the north of New Guinea without investigating the main group.

Abel Janszoon Tasman was next, on 19th January 1643. Thirteen days out of New Zealand he came upon a small high island which looked like the breasts of a woman, and named it Hooge Pijlstaerts, usually simplified to Pylstart, but now known by its Tongan name of 'Ata. Next he came to Eua and Tonga-tapu, which he named Middelburch and Amsterdam; and here he and his men made many friendly contacts with the people, exchanging nails, knives, and cloth for pigs, fish, fowls, yams, and bananas.

After his spectacular discovery of Tahiti, Captain Samuel Wallis came to Tafahi and Niuatoputapu in 1767.

But it was left to Captain Cook to give us our best descriptions of the islands he named "Friendly". In October 1773 he landed at Eua and Tonga-tapu, observing that the houses were surrounded with sweet-smelling flowers, and that the food gardens were set out in rows. He commented on the love of singing and dancing the islanders displayed, the juggling and the games.

Cook went on to New Zealand, returning nine months later, but on this occasion he called only at Nomuka, in the central group of Ha'apai. He returned to Nomuka on his third voyage at the end of April 1777, and was met by Finau Ulukalala, the powerful ruler of Vava'u; a man whose physical prowess amazed the British. Finau invited

Cook to Lifuka, and there entertained him with such a feast as that great traveller had never seen, with dancing and with songs. Wrestling and boxing contests intrigued Cook; women and children as well as men took part; and he noted that the boxing differed very little from the sport as practised in England.

"Some of our people ventured to contend with them in both exercises, but were always worsted; except in a few instances, where it appeared that the fear they were in of offending us contributed more to the victory than the superiority of the persons so engaged."

The feast, however, was a stratagem; Finau's purpose was to kill the voyagers and seize the ships and guns. He differed with his supporting chiefs on the details of whether the attack would be made by night or by day and, either in a fit of pique or in a very real doubt of the successful issue of the plan, called the whole thing off. Cook lived to be killed in Hawaii on the same voyage, on 14th February 1779. He never knew that the friendliness for which he named Lifuka and the whole Tongan group was camouflage for a projected act of treachery.

If this episode scarcely fits the reputation that Tongans enjoyed for peace-loving courtesy, the answer is to be found in another foreign contact. About twenty years before Cook's arrival, approximately in the year 1750, the young men from the northern Tongan groups especially began to sail to Fiji, adventure bound. They were never disappointed.

At any time some Fijians were at war with others, and the Tongans could always make an alliance with a chief ready to conduct an expedition against his neighbours. Of superior physical build, unafraid, and all of them volunteers, the Tongans could usually ensure the victory; and they were rewarded by gifts of what they most desired— the Fijian canoes.

These were the most impressive nautical constructions in the whole Pacific; in many ways they were superior at that time to any other navigable vessels in the world. Longer than the ships of the European explorers who encountered them, they carried more men in their crews. They were not properly canoes, but great double-hulled vessels with sewn planks and self-reefing sails. They pointed up much closer to the wind than any European vessel of the time; some have reported them as sailing within three points (or 34 degrees) of the wind, displaying an incredible efficiency. They tacked by reversing; as a result they carried steering-oars at either end; for in the speed of the manoeuvre a single oar could not be taken to its new position. Some of these oars have been measured at 34 feet in length; they took seven men to control them; and the complements of the canoes have been tallied at one hundred and fifty. Moreover, they were faster than anything else on the ocean; when they were replaced eventually by the European-type schooner it was not on any score of greater efficiency, but simply as a matter of economics: the construction and management of such vessels involved the labour of a great many men, and ownership was therefore possible only to the greatest of the chiefs.

The Tongan canoes were lesser vessels, with crews of up to fifty men; for the Tongans did not have in their own islands the reserves of heavy timber available to the Fijians. The reward of a canoe was a tremendous incitement to men who fought the wars of a country not their own.

But the mercenaries—and Finau Ulukalala was amongst them—learned a terrible intoxication in their Fijian engagements, the intoxication of savagery, replacing their previous pride in military skill. They learned cannibalism and the vindictive torture of prisoners; they abandoned such refinements of martial procedure as had hitherto characterized their engagements, and conceived a thirst for blood and bloodletting.

Finau also became obsessed with the idea of controlling all Tonga, an obsession he transmitted to his descendants. It was from these contacts with the Fijians that the Tongans inherited a series of internecine wars that ravaged the islands until, through inheritance, they were united under the first Tongan King, and for the first time the regions of Ha'apai, Vava'u, and Tonga looked to a single ruler. It was Taufa'ahau Tupou who, in admiration of George III of England, took that monarch's name to himself and named his wife after George III's consort, Charlotte (which in Tongan is Salote).

This history was handed down verbally to each new generation of Tongans, but a good deal of it is duplicated (and thus authenticated) by the account of William Mariner, a thirteen-year-old lad who sailed from London in February 1805 on the privateer *Port-au-Prince*, 466 tons, Captain Isaac Duck commanding. Two years of fairly savage raiding combined with whaling and sealing brought her to Tonga, where she fell victim to Finau's son, who had the same name and rank as his father, as well as the same savagery and ambition.

Mariner escaped from the general slaughter because Finau liked the looks of him; he became a protégé of the chief, and at a later stage, tattooed like a Tongan, he acquired the status of a chief. He returned to London in 1811, and his account of his adventures, transcribed by a Dr John Martin and checked by him against the memories of another survivor, is one of the most authentic pictures of the early Pacific ever presented to the public.

Mariner became a London accountant, and afterwards a stockbroker. Though he had survived all kinds of perils in the Pacific, becoming a noted swimmer in the process, he met his death by drowning in the River Thames in 1853.

When the Free Church of Tonga acquired the *Ilex* she was rechristened by Queen Salote, and thereafter sailed under the name *Tu'uakitau*. This was a proud nickname of the Queen's ancestor, George Tupou I; and the rechristening can be taken as an earnest of the respect with which the Tongans welcomed this addition to the tiny island fleet.

A story current in the islands relates that when George Tupou was born and the navel cord was cut, it was buried under an ironwood tree, following the custom of burying the cord in a significant place, a place that would lend its reputed character to the baby. This ironwood at Ha'apai had the name Tu'uakitau. The timber produced by the ironwood tree is that from which Tongan war-clubs were made, and George Tupou's father hoped that his son would be the weapon to unite all Tonga, as in time to come he was. The translation of the name, "He can stand and fight", may also be given as "Endure through fighting" or, perhaps, "Challenge".

Another story is that it is the name of a tall tree in Ha'apai, a tree where George Tupou made his resolution to bring all Tonga under one flag and one rule. There are other versions, and probably all of them contain some truth.

It is a proud name in Tonga. Taufa'ahau Tupou was born in 1797, and grew to be a man of exceptional height and strength, a leader in sport and war, and a nautical expert whose feats and abilities amazed this nation of sea-farers. In 1820 he succeeded to the rule of Ha'apai. In 1833 Finau Ulukalala IV entrusted him with Vava'u as regent until the child successor should be fit. The successor died, and Taufa'ahau retained command. In 1845, by a mixture of inheritance and nomination, he succeeded in the dignity of Tui Kanokupolu, the ruler of Tonga-tapu. He thus united under a single rule the three parts of Tonga; though it was a few more years before he finally controlled some of the more recalcitrant chiefs.

The Methodist missionaries had come to Tonga in 1822. Taufa'ahau Tupou was immediately attracted to the Christian creed, and was baptized in 1831, taking the name George at that time. In this year the first books were printed in Tongan by the missionaries. By 1839 George Tupou had the Vava'u Code of Laws printed, and this was the first written code in Tonga. In 1850 a similar code was produced for the whole of the Tongan group. In 1855 George made a treaty with the French, in 1876 with Germany, in 1879 with Great Britain, and in 1888 with the United States. In each of these recognition of Tongan independence was a major provision.

In 1862 George set up the first Parliament. In 1875 a Tongan Constitution laid the foundation of the present legal and administrative system of Tonga, and to this day, with its amendments, remains the law of the land.

"It is my wish," George told the 1875 Parliament, "to grant a Constitution and to carry on my duties in accordance with it, and those that come after me shall do the same, and the Constitution shall be a firm rock in Tonga forever. When the Constitution has been passed it shall be a palladium of freedom to Tongans forever. It is quite clear now that they are free; and let this be the most valuable privilege of the country, for by the passing of the Constitution a Tongan can boast that he is as free as were the Romans of former days, and as the British are now."

It was with pride that the *Ilex* wore the appelation of such a monarch; but the moment of the rechristening seemed shortly to have been the highlight of the cutter's life; a life that hereafter headed towards oblivion.

For a ship to prosper she must complement a man; a man of that particular kind that needs a ship. Owner, captain, charterer, that makes no difference; there must be a sympathetic human intelligence to feel the vicissitudes endured by canvas and timber. The captains of the Free Church were either replaced too quickly or they were inadequate to the needs of the *Tu'uakitau*; she began to deteriorate, as though she felt in her proud and ageing heart a certain ignominy in the loss of her "yacht" status.

For a yacht is a vessel that is not hired or chartered, a vessel not used in trade or commerce, nor in the necessities of war; and the *Tu'uakitau* found herself converted to the purposes of the Mission; now running with cargoes of copra or coconut or supplies for outstations, now in the transfer of Mission personnel.

She began to deteriorate in all her particulars; her running rigging was renewed only as necessity dictated, her standing rigging was questionable; such of her paintwork as remained called for the blowtorch rather than the brush; her decks and housings deteriorated beyond repair, and her canvas was good only for the best of weather.

In profile, and at a little distance, she was a proud ship still; she looked a picture as she lay in the boat-harbour a mile or two westward from Nuku'alofa, where she compared, and usually to advantage, with the cruising yachts that criss-cross the Pacific and seldom fail to make a temporary haven of Tonga. She served nine years with the church, and in that time few replacements went to the preservation of her self-respect.

She had her adventures in that time, and nearly came to grief in the first year of her church ownership when a hurricane drove her off her normal moorings in Ha'apai nearly 400 miles to the remote island of Ono-i-Lau in the Southern Fijis.

In 1957 she was put up for sale, and bought by Tofa Ramsay. By this time she had so far deteriorated that, in spite of a world-wide inflation which touched even this remote outpost, she brought no more than £2,000; the equivalent of £1,600 sterling.

Tofa, a European with a Tongan practicality, thought "Stand and Fight" was no name for a vessel practically on her last legs. A translation from the colourful language, full of similes and metaphors, which Tongans use for normal speech could mean "Challenge"; a challenge either to a fight or a foot-race; and the elderly *Ilex* by no means measured up to it. Ramsay rechristened her with the sardonic rhyme "Tuaikaepau"—"Slow but sure"; and at the same time set about doing what he could to restore her former glory.

He put in a new Lister diesel engine at a cost of £1,275; and spent another £350 on a rebuilding operation which brought her decking and deck-housing up to standard. He sailed her to Auckland for these repairs, which he carried out as he could finance them. He also spent another £187 on sails and rigging.

Tofa is a slim-built fellow whose oilskins, as the saying goes, have shed more salt-water than a good many people have ever seen. Outwardly shy and retiring, he has the confidence of the seaman; he knows he can hold his own in his own sort of company. He passes as European, though on his mother's side he is Tongan. Nevertheless his English is halting; he prefers the Polynesian tongue even though this means communicating through an interpreter. His normal engagement is in the local coasting trade round Tonga, where the produce of every island must be collected by small boats, and where the handling of such boats takes a good deal of enterprise and ingenuity because of the coral masses. "Tofa" means "good-bye". It is a good name for a seaman; though it has a wry applicability for a shipmaster who has just lost a ship.

Tofa has another, smaller ship, the *Taufale*; she is a good vessel in good order, but the *Tuaikaepau* was the pride of his heart.

31

Tofa's father, Stuart Ramsay, was a figure of romance, even in the romantic Pacific. Tofa himself knows of him only that he was the original "Tin Can swimmer", and that he wrote a book.

For a number of years Stuart Ramsay, a young fellow out from England, kept a store in Niuafo'ou, more frequently nowadays called Tin Can Island, a name for which Ramsay claims responsibility. The island is girt by a coast so rough that in all but exceptional weather not even canoes can effect a landing. It carried, however, a considerable population, which Ramsay went to serve. The store was possible because, under favourable conditions, a boat may be laid close enough to a ledge of rock at one side of the island to allow passengers to jump and goods to be thrown ashore.

The fishermen of Niuafo'ou had long before evolved their own method of exploiting the deep waters close to the island. They swam, wearing a kind of bamboo lifebelt and pushing a large bamboo ahead of them for a float. When they came to their selected spot they trod water, and from a net bag slung over their shoulders produced lines, being supported more than ordinarily high in the sea by the bamboo jacket. The fish they caught went into the bag.

There were sharks in plenty; but they worried the islanders not at all; indeed, most Tongans have a complete faith in their ability to survive in a shark-infested sea; and survive, for some unknown reason, they do. In the bay whaling which still, in Tonga, is carried out with sailing-boats and hand-held harpoons, the death-blow is frequently delivered by a crew member who runs up on the whale's back for a better aim. The flurry almost as frequently unseats him; and at this stage the sea may be boiling with the urgencies of sharks excited by the prospect of the feast to come, or already slashing into the flesh of the doomed whale.

The scanty mail for Niuafo'ou had, in Ramsay's time, frequently been delivered by rocket from the ship *Tofua*, a method infuriating to the islanders, for the flame of the rocket frequently set fire to the packet, or delivered it into some thicket where it could not be found. Ramsay began the practice of swimming with the mail.

Captain Davey, of the *Tofua*, perceived a publicity value in the practice; tourists were intrigued by it. Mail for delivery ashore was put into a tin can, and in a short while special stamps were printed for Niuafo'ou, and marked "Tin Can Mail". Philatelists rushed the issues, and the little island had all the mail it could handle. A respectable sum swelled Tongan coffers.

Ramsay later wrote a book about his life on Niuafo'ou, in which he claimed that he had swum with the monthly mail 112 times. Others have claimed to have been the first postmen; but photographs and documents reproduced in Ramsay's book, *Tin Can Mail*, attest to its validity.

The island, a rock 588 feet high, is a weird and beautiful spot, characterized by old lava flows and craters of its several volcanic outlets. It has a large central lake and several smaller ones. In 1853 a volcanic eruption killed twenty-five people, and there were other eruptions in 1867, 1886, 1912, 1929, 1935, and 1946. After the last the population was moved to the large fertile island of Eua; and for several subsequent years Niuafo'ou was visited only by copra-cutters, who were relieved every few months. Recently a few families have been given permission to return to live in their old village of Angaha.

Ramsay's son Tofa was born in Ha'apai in 1917, and now lives in a fine two-storeyed home in Nuku'alofa. He has owned a number of schooners. His first, the *Hifofua*, still trades today in Fiji under the name *Maroro*. He has been sailing all his life, and he has a reputation for seamanship.

Not long before the *Tuaikaepau* was lost Tofa was aboard his 42-foot cutter *Taufale* in Ha'afeva Harbour, in Ha'apai. His regular skipper, Ve'etutu Pahulu, was with him when they heard a hurricane warning on the radio. Most of the other small boats in harbour were pulled up on the beach; but that, in such hurricanes as the Friendly Islands experience, is sometimes a waste of effort. Tofa decided to ride the storm out.

They were then in fairly shallow water. They set out all their anchors and, to ensure their holding, drilled holes in the coral bottom to take the flukes. Two of his crew were ashore, but the third man, Sione Fatafehi, stayed with them. They were lying off a lee shore. A government ship, the *Fangailefuka*, pulled up her anchors and steamed to the far side of the island, where she was not only run up on the beach but moored there with heavy anchors dug in on the land and lines run to the palms. A small ship which was assigned in its normal duties to the Governor of Ha'apai, the *Fangailefuka* was beautifully modern with remote controls worked from the bridge. Besides the Governor, she carried the doctor on his medical rounds.

"Ve'etutu carried out all my orders with the heart of a lion," Tofa has said. "When the hurricane developed we had to run the engines with great judgment, to keep a steady strain on the anchor chains; and all the time we had to steer into the teeth of the wind. But the anchor cables held. Once the storm had reached its greatest force we had the engines running full speed; they ran like that for hours, from the late evening until seven in the morning."

At three in the morning, by the illumination of lightning flashes, they saw the houses ashore melting away; just disintegrating in the wind. Some time late in the morning they lost their rudder, but by then they were safe.

34

The boats that had been pulled ashore, as well as every other in the harbour, were smashed to pieces. The *Fangailefuka*, despite anchor chains and fastenings and the grip of her keel on the ground, was pushed off the beach where she sheltered behind the island, and no trace of her has yet been found.

Tofa went back to his usual avocation, carrying stores for some of the big companies to their branches on the smaller islands, and returning with cargoes of copra or coconuts or both. With his two ships he had worked up a good business; Ve'etutu was his captain. But whenever the *Tuaikaepau* sailed Tofa went with her; he had fallen in love with her and hardly trusted her out of his hands.

"I was so confident that she'd go anywhere, any time, I'd sail her into the teeth of a hurricane and it wouldn't worry me," he has said. "I've had her in bad weather. First time I took her to New Zealand we struck some really heavy stuff on the return. I had to pull the sails right off her. Then we set them again, reefed right down; and she went as sweet as a bird."

The trip to New Zealand had a double purpose. Tofa needed repairs done in a good yard; and he also had the idea of searching out likely crew members for a projected voyage round the world. The *Tuaikaepau* sailed on 3rd March 1962, with a total complement of ten. They tried then to call in at 'Ata, on the way south, but the extremely rough weather persuaded them to abandon that plan; and they took thirteen days, sailing direct from Nuku'alofa to Rangitoto in Waitemata Harbour, Auckland.

They left Auckland on 2nd June, and made the return trip in nine days, assisted by winds of a velocity up to 65 knots. They attempted to make a stay at Raoul Island in the Kermadecs, but this proved impossible in the weather prevailing. They anchored off 'Ata, though, in the evening of the eighth day, and fished for two hours, catching fifteen tuna, of which the smallest weighed ninety pounds. On the ninth day they reached Nuku'alofa, where crowds gathered to welcome them.

Tofa was delighted with the *Tuaikaepau's* performance on this voyage. At best he could get about nine knots out of her. She sailed very well into the wind; while she was on her best course she took a little wash over the stern; but if she were tucked up as close to the wind as possible she remained a dry ship.

For the New Zealand voyage, neither Tofa's qualifications nor Ve'etutu Pahulu's were sufficient, and Tofa hired the man who was regarded as the best captain in the islands, Tevita (David) Fifita. He had a Tongan foreign-going master's certificate as well as a mate's in the New Zealand registry; not only that, but he was a man who radiated confidence. He was one of Tonga's best-known personalities, and one of the most admired.

Though Tofa accompanied him on his first voyage, he was prepared to put David Fifita in sole charge of the second without any qualms. There was to be a larger complement; plenty of Tongans, particularly Tongan boxers, were keen to visit Auckland, for Tongans are beginning to feel their confinement on their islands. Such men could live on the ship for an absurdly small sum; by getting seasonal work, as in a meat-freezing works, they could make a small fortune (by Tongan standards) in short order, and save most of it. In July a second voyage set out.

"As for disaster, I didn't think it was possible," Tofa said. "I didn't believe anything could happen to those men. If navigation and ship-handling weren't perfect, then I'd say that David Fifita must have been washed overboard; and I didn't think that could happen either. If David was safe my ship was safe; and that was all. That's the confidence I had in him."

Chapter Three

DAVID FIFITA is a man who inspires confidence; there are
not many who have this attribute in such a high degree. He
is a large man, over six feet in height, and for years before
the voyage of the *Tuaikaepau* was carrying too much
weight at his normal 288 pounds. Tonga admires a big man,
as it admires an efficient sea captain; and a confusion between size and stature could perhaps be described as a
Tongan national failing; though it is true that often enough,
as with Fifita, size and stature will go together.

More likely it is a certain steadiness of bearing, a certain
confidence that illumines his face, an observable speed in
sizing up a situation and acting on it, the reflection of intelligence and the calm of a pair of remarkable eyes that
combine to produce this effect upon the observer. Moreover, Fifita is a handsome man; he has the national characteristic of neatness and cleanliness in dress and body, his
movements are smoothly articulated, and he has a firm,
pleasant voice, moderately pitched.

His eyes would be his most remarkable feature. They are a seaman's eyes, framed in lids that show the effect of sea-glare; eyes that have pitched upon sky and ocean more frequently and familiarly than on the green heart of the land. Captain A. J. C. Tippett, who once commanded the inter-island steamer *Aoniu,* on which David was mate, comments not on his eyes but on his eyesight, which, he says, was amazing.

"Especially at night. He could see like a cat in the dark, and the detail he could describe accurately was remarkable," he says.

David must have been able to inspire this confidence from an early age. When he was eleven he was unofficially commanding a schooner on short trips—as, for example, the hundred miles between Nuku'alofa and Ha'apai. By the time he was eighteen he was a qualified master.

His faults, which are not obvious, stem from a self-confidence that is, perhaps, a little excessive; he has been known to display symptoms of vanity, and there is no doubt at all that he could, in certain circumstances, be ruthless.

David Fifita was born in Lifuka, the largest island of Ha'apai, on 28th November 1919, to become the eldest of eight children. Of the other seven, four were boys. Laitia is head of the Weather Department in Nuku'alofa; Pita (Peter) is skipper of a fishing-boat there, Tolati is captain of the government vessel *Kao*, a landing-barge that services the islands; and Sione (Johnny), the youngest, looks after the family coconut plantations and gardens. In a country in which only three per cent of the population are employed (and two of the three are employees of Government) this is a fine family record.

David is sometimes nicknamed "Fisi", meaning Fiji. (The Fiji Islands got their name from the inability of Tongans to pronounce "Viti", which in Fijian means "island". The inability of European whalers to pronounce or recognize these sounds converted them to "Feegee" and "Fejee" and through a dozen other variations to a final "Fiji".) From this circumstance it is said that David's father, Semesi Fifita, was Fijian, but David denies this and says that if there is an admixture of Fijian blood in his inheritance it is very small. Certainly "Fisi" has been a Ha'apai nickname for a century and a half, as Mariner's book testifies.

David went to primary school at Lifuka, and continued his studies at Apifo'ou Catholic College in Nuku'alofa. When he left school, in March 1937, he was seventeen, and in July of that year he shipped as a hand on his father's schooner *Malolelei*, a name which is a greeting in Tonga, is sometimes translated "Good morning", but more literally means "Thank you for being well".

In the following year David secured his Home Trade Master's Certificate, a coasting certificate of command which ensured him a career. The studies normally take three years, and the applicant is supposed to have an experience of at least this time at sea. But David was a bright lad, he knew his trade very well and could pass the examinations, and some official eyes were winked as his application went through.

A year after that his father wanted to retire from the sea and pay full attention to his garden. He relinquished the *Malolelei* to David, but retained a connection with the sea by skippering, from time to time as his services were needed, a small Catholic Mission vessel, *Fetu'u Moana* (Star of the Ocean).

From 1943 to 1947 David commanded the *Oliv*; from that he went to the Free Church's *Tu'uakitau*, his first connection with the ship with which his name will ever be linked. He was mate on the *Aoniu*, then captain of the *Hifofua*, then mate on the *Aoniu* again.

At an early stage of his career he came under the notice of Karl Johnson, a naturalized New Zealander who had the name "Schroder" tattooed on his chest. Johnson was a captain who had qualified while serving with the German four-masters which used to trade with South America. He had been round the Horn under sail, and was a practical man with a love for nautical mathematics. He taught two of the Tongan lads, David Fifita and George Walters; and these two quickly established reputations as being the Tongan small-ship skippers best qualified to navigate. Johnson used to say that Fifita learnt more quickly and had a better head for figures; at that time, however, Johnson was inclined to put more trust in Walters.

But David from childhood had been accustomed to the responsibility of ship-handling; and from childhood too he had been accustomed to disaster, to self-control in emergencies, and to the required or indicated action. He was only eleven years old when, one day in 1931, he was sent to the island of Foa with his uncle Epalahame (Abraham) to bring a boat back. A sudden storm they encountered on their return to their home port of Pangai, on the island of Lifuka, drove them out of their course, but they managed to beach the boat on the island of Lofanga without sustaining any damage.

This was high adventure for a schoolboy, but in the following year he encountered a still greater danger. He was sailing with a man named Fonua and three younger lads from the island of Uoleva to Pangai when their boat sank under them. The group swam to a reef known as Haukalea, where there was a lighthouse, and there they remained, alongside the light, until they were picked up by the cutter *Uini*, and taken home.

In 1941, after David had secured his Home Master's Certificate, he was caught in a hurricane with 106 schoolchildren aboard his vessel. He ran to the island of 'Ata, a hundred miles south of Tonga, and stayed there eight days. Always prepared for an emergency, he was able to feed the children for the period. He reached Pangai on New Year's Eve, with everyone safe, and probably at this time began to engender the confidence that, throughout his life, everyone reposed in him.

On 3rd October 1955 David was commanding the *Aoniu* and struck a pack of trouble. An engine breakdown forced him to anchor at Niuafo'ou, the Tin Can Island, and under the strain of heavy winds his anchor-chain broke. His radio transmitter complicated the situation by choosing that moment to go out of commission, and he was unable to get in touch with Tonga or with any source of likely assistance. Under sails improvised from tarpaulins he got way on the ship and drove with the wind behind him for Fiji. With fifty-eight passengers aboard he felt the weight of the responsibility vested in him; in Suva he hove to on the spot where vessels are required to wait for customs clearance and inspection.

At the time of his enforced departure from Niuafo'ou, on the same day and at approximately the same hour, the motor vessel *Joyita*, on which David had served briefly as mate, was leaving Apia in Western Samoa for the Tokelaus, with a crew of fourteen and eleven passengers. On 10th November *Joyita* was discovered abandoned, waterlogged and partly submerged ninety miles north of the Fiji group, and the mystery of the disappearance of her complement has never been solved.

In 1956 David, as captain of the *Aoniu*, was caught in a violent storm between New Zealand and Raoul Island in the Kermadecs. He was taking government cargo to Raoul; and though he lost his deck cargo and his vessel was badly damaged he carried out what was, even in normal weather, a hazardous commission, and made a successful delivery.

In the following year he was again caught in a storm between New Zealand and Fiji. Again there was no loss of life, but severe damage had to be repaired in Suva.

Four years before that, in October 1953, while David was running cargoes in the *Hifofua* for Tofa Ramsay, his father Semesi took eight lads out fishing in a 20-foot cutter, the *Filimeipulotu*. The vessel foundered in moderately heavy weather, and left them in the sea between the islands of Fotuhaa and Kao; at approximately the same spot as saw Captain William "Breadfruit" Bligh set adrift with eighteen men in a 23-foot open boat by the mutineers of H.M.S. *Bounty*, in April 1789.

This was eight miles from the island of Fotuhaa, ten from Kao; but Semesi Fifita told his charges to swim the longer distance. For one thing, there was a heavy wind blowing and a fairly large sea; to swim to Kao would keep the wind and the sea behind them and lighten their task. For another, Semesi knew that his son David would be passing down-channel in the *Hifofua* later that night; and would intersect the line the swimmers would take.

Semesi sent the five best swimmers ahead, telling them that he and the others would come on slowly. After an hour and a half in the water he drowned. He used his last energies to impress on his three young companions that David's ship would cross their path. He knew David's plans from a meeting three days before.

The darkness came down, and the three lads went on. To their joy they saw the riding-lights of a small ship approaching; they swam as hard as they could to intersect its track, shouting as they came in close. They were so near they could see the men on the deck; but in the noise and confusion of a sailing-ship in a stiff breeze their cries went unheard. For sailing-ships are not the quiet ghosts a later generation believes them to be; even in the cold grey stillness of a fog there is a slap of blocks against spars or rigging, the occasional rolling of some unsecured object, unexplained noises from unknown sources. In the wind the rigging cracks like a wielded whip, masts creak and timbers groan, the wind moans in the harp of shrouds, and the seas drum on the hull. In storm the ear rejects noise; there is so much of it, and so much is meaningless.

The swimming lads were close enough to recognize David on the deck, but they could not attract his attention. Two of them reached the shore; the five swimmers who preceded them were never seen again.

The tragedy of his father's death was heightened for David by his own proximity at the time. Like most of his race he has a strong sense of family; the night of his father's death remains vivid for him. In a small community like Tonga a loss of seven lives assumes the proportions of a national tragedy; and the report that Semesi hoped to the last for David's intervention enhanced his sense of loss.

David himself married at the age of eighteen. His wife, Alapasita, also came from Ha'apai—"Ha'apai girls are best," David says with a Lothario grin. They had a family of seven girls, and two boys: Sateki, the eldest of the family, and a young one, born in 1954.

The Lothario description is not unjustified. David, like a majority of Tongans, has a weakness or, depending on the point of view, a passion for dalliance that seems quite unchecked by his very sincere religious faith. He is a Roman Catholic; and, like most of his fellow countrymen, he is influenced by his religion in every aspect of his life.

In part, this Tongan attitude is dictated by certain features of the environment. For example, everyone on these fortunate islands is literate; but there is little, indeed, for them to read. Their literacy is in a language that has a currency of no more than, perhaps, eighty thousand participators: the islanders themselves and certain others who live in Fiji or Samoa. There is a great hunger for reading-matter in Tonga; the daily news-sheet produced by the Government attracts queues of readers to the notice-boards where it is displayed; but there is no other newspaper, and the lack of general literature is a little frightening.

In these circumstances every Tongan knows his Bible well and reads with avidity everything produced by the missions. His belief, if he is an average citizen, is sincere and total; but much of his thought is concentrated in religious avenues because of the lack of other reading-matter. A language of their own is a great, and perhaps intolerable, luxury for a people so limited in numbers; and a literature so specialized keeps national ideas too narrowly channelled.

Moreover, the social life of the islands is such that the Sunday church service is a highlight. There are other occasions for dancing and singing; but the Tongan is a social being, gregarious and happy in the company of his fellows. Church attendances are phenomenally high. Again, a contribution to this circumstance has been made by the Sunday observance laws, which are strict: probably far more strict than in any other Christian community on earth. A brother of mine, a doctor long resident in these islands, was fined for cutting a bunch of bananas in his own Ha'apai garden on a Sunday. No work is possible, nor any amusement; and church attendance has become the big social occasion of the week.

Among the more sophisticated Tongans a condition is growing in which the forms of religion have become more important, perhaps, than its deeper content; but such an observation would not apply to David Fifita; nor to more than a very small percentage of the population. David feels the very solid assurance he gets from his faith; he is a friend of his "body-saint", St Joseph, and he has a staunch belief in the realities of religion. It is his hope that one of his daughters will become a nun. He has a great comfort from the blessings of his creed.

He has the Polynesian attribute of being able to speak well; oratory has always been one of the highest arts of this cultivated race, and David has the assurance and the intelligence that a good exponent requires. He has something of a gift of tongues; he speaks excellent Fijian and accurate Samoan. Though Samoan and Tongan may be described as dialects of the same language, and many of the words are the same, there are subtle differences in meaning and usage. David also speaks good English; he writes it, too, in a rather stilted fashion; but in any verbal communication of import he prefers to use an interpreter.

Between jobs, and in slack seasons, he has acted as pilot for strange vessels entering the ports of Vava'u, Ha'apai, and Nuku'alofa. For one period of six months, while the Harbour Master at Nuku'alofa was on long leave, he assumed that position.

In March 1962, when Tofa Ramsay was going to take his *Tuaikaepau* to New Zealand for repairs, he called on David, as holder of a foreign-going master's certificate, to skipper the expedition. Besides her regular crew she carried a number of Tongans signed on as crewmen; these included a boxer or two, anxious to pick up some fights and some fight money in Auckland, and others who merely wanted to see something of the world.

For them, once they had secured passage, it was easy to make the trip pay. They could live well on the foodstuffs, the taro and yams and lily-stems, that the ship carried from Tonga; and pick up seasonal work in Auckland, to return richer than they had left, with their passage money paid. They were so successful that, with the prospect of another voyage ahead, Tofa was besieged with applications. He insisted on the money, £43, being paid in advance; but there were some privileged passengers who managed to persuade him to defer his charges until such time as they should have earned the money.

Counting David, there were seven in the regular crew, but there were ten who ranked, unofficially, as passengers.

Of the amount of £430, Tofa had been paid £105 by the time they left. David had also received some money, but had spent most of it in provisioning and fuelling the ship. He had about £7 left; and this was all the wealth the ship carried, except for minute amounts in the pockets of one or two passengers.

Captain J. T. Sutherland, Port Captain of Nuku'alofa, had been impressed by the work carried out on the ship, and retained misgivings on only two points. The first was that the quality of the housing roof above the coamings was not all he felt it ought to be. The second was that the ship had no bulkheads; the whole of her interior was open. The exceptionally strong construction of the diagonal skin was reinforced, as is usual, by long timbers running the full length of the ship; she had no ribbing, but the longitudinal stringers and plates were ample; and then she had weathered the storms of more than half a century.

In addition to David Fifita, in whom he had absolute confidence, Tofa was pleased that Ve'etutu Pahulu, with whom he had ridden out the hurricane in the *Hifofua*, was going along as second-in-command.

Two of David's sons were on the voyage, Sateki Fifita, the eldest of the captain's regular family and, at twenty-two, the centre of his hopes; and an illegitimate son, Talo Fifita (or Lopeka). Talo is a smooth-faced, almost a baby-faced, boy. He normally wears a slight moustache which does nothing to make him look more mature; and it comes as something of a shock to learn that he is married and the father of three children; and that for five years before this voyage he had been making a living as crew member of the inter-island steamer *Aoniu*, and in other maritime jobs.

The ship's carpenter was another David, Tevita Uaisele, a married man with eight children. The engineer was Fine Feuiaki, and the remaining crew member was Sione (or Johnny) Lousi, whose age was thirty.

Since money is not easily come by in Tonga, and the ability to pay passage to New Zealand is an idle dream for most, the passengers were men of some substance, though for the most part they were young. The eldest was Fatai Efiafi, a widower aged forty-six. He seemed more or less at a loose end.

Also in his forties, but a little younger, was Sione Vai-angina Unga, a copra planter who, with considerable industry, managed plantations rather larger than the ordinary Tongan holding. He had previously never had anything to do with the sea, except as a passenger on the short trips of a couple of hundred miles between Vava'u and Nuku'-alofa. He is the father of seven children, the eldest aged twenty-one, and is a follower of the Mormon creed.

Viliame Fa'onuku, usually known as William Fa, was a bachelor of thirty-four years of age, and a notably good carpenter. His projected trip to New Zealand was simply for the purpose of seeing something of the world. A quiet, unassuming fellow, and small as Tongans go, he has an engaging personality which shows to advantage only after a considerable acquaintance.

Teiapa'a Bloomfield, a young fellow about twenty-three, was a taxi-driver; a profession which, in Tonga, has been in the money since the Americans started using the Central Pacific for their atomic blasts; for considerable parties of Americans on notable and apparently uninvestigated expense accounts have been assigned to Tonga, as to other islands, to make scientific observations.

Teiapa'a was notable among Tongans, or Polynesians anywhere, for the simple fact that he was unable to swim. Though the taxi business his father owns has its garage only a hundred yards or so from the sea, he had never been interested in the water or the shores. He had been a wild youth, more than a little unruly.

His purpose in visiting New Zealand was, he says, to

47

investigate the drinking facilities. He knew of it as a land where the hotels stayed open throughout the day; and Teiapa'a never missed a good chance of indulging his taste for alcohol. Tonga has no hotels, and liquor parties, when they exist, are by arrangement for those who are not members of the rather exclusive clubs.

On this matter Teiapa'a fell out with his father; shortly before the *Tuaikaepau* sailed from Faa'ua, the boat harbour of Nuku'alofa, he came back into the city to say good-bye. But his father, Sunia (Junior) Bloomfield, was angry with him; he said that he was finished with Teiapa'a and washed his hands of him, for he thought of nothing but drinking and going about with wild companions. He would no longer regard Teiapa'a as a son of his, he said; Teiapa'a could do what he liked and go where he wished.

At the time these strictures meant little to Teiapa'a. He replied to them rudely, and went on his way back to the ship.

The other members of the ship's complement were all boxers, most of them forming a troupe under the management of Soakai Pulu. One of the most respected and popular men in Tonga, Soakai is a handsome man with aristocratic features and a gift for thoughtful and intelligent speech. He was born on 16th December 1910. In 1934 he won the heavyweight boxing championship of Tonga from a man named Faha'ivale, and held the title undefeated until 1953, when he retired and began to train youngsters in the sport. In that time, however, he had fought three times in Fiji for the Fijian championship, in 1934, 1936, and 1947; but on each occasion he was defeated.

His son, Fetaiaki Pulu, was also something of a boxer, and Soakai hoped to get fights for him in New Zealand. He also had hopes for fellow-passenger Sione (Johnny) Sikimeti, who at eighteen was a promising young lad with a nice style.

The current heavyweight and light-heavy champion of Tonga was another passenger. He was Sipa Fine Sekona, a well-built twenty-year-old from Fo'ui, a village on the western side of the main island of Tonga. Sipa had been to New Zealand before, in 1959, and in the course of an extended stay of about a year he had fought twice, winning both bouts decisively, the first on a knock-out in the first round, the second on a technical knock-out in the third. In his Tongan experience Sipa had fought every boxer of note and been successful. He is a handsome lad with an expressive, intelligent face.

Accompanying Sipa was his cousin, seventeen-year-old Finau Laione Sekona, from the same village. Finau fought at about 134 pounds, and hoped to get a couple of bouts at his weight in New Zealand. He looked years younger than his age, and he was on his first sea voyage. He was to become a kind of mascot for the crew; Sipa looked after him, but Finau earned the affectionate regard of everyone else on board.

The last of the boxers was Saia Peni. He had been to New Zealand on the earlier voyage of the *Tuaikaepau*, from March until June of 1962. He had a fight, on that visit, with a half-caste Raratongan; he was knocked out in the first round, but nevertheless had made arrangements for other engagements. As a boxer he was entirely un-trained; he had just taken up the sport because of a liking for it and some facility; he had matched himself with other men, but had never had a trainer, or other assistance.

Saia was a member of a chief's family, and other Tongans therefore expected from him a standard of conduct rather higher than he had been willing to give, for he had been a rebel all his life. He had always reacted strongly against discipline; and from his childhood the elders of the village had found occasion to deprecate his behaviour, in view of his family connections. His uncle, in his village (the large village of Kolonga, from which Soakai and his son also came), bears the title of "nuku", or chief.

With such a passenger list, it was natural that the people of Tonga took an intense interest in the sailing of the *Tuaikaepau*. Boxing has always been a sport highly regarded, right down into the mists of Tongan history. Moreover, in those islands there is a special veneration for the good carpenter; and the *Tuaikaepau* carried two carpenters, David Uaisele and William Fa. Captain Fifita was a popular and respected figure, and his *mana* extended to both his sons, Sateki and Talo. Ve'etutu had his own proud reputation, as, of a different sort, did Vaiangina. It would have been hard to arrange an expedition with more public idols than the *Tuaikaepau* carried.

There was no urgency about the voyage. David planned a dawn landfall at 'Ata, an island south of Tonga-tapu, more or less on the direct route to New Zealand; and they thought they would spend a day there, perhaps two or three days, fishing and investigating the island. But they were dogged from the beginning with manifestations of bad luck such as might have disturbed seamen of a race more given to superstition.

They began their passage from Faa'ua using only the engine, and had gone a considerable way before they discovered that they had no electric torch aboard. There was, indeed, no electricity of any sort on the *Tuaikaepau*. In an earlier day this certainly would not have worried them; but light had become essential; a torch for reading the compass and for the hundred and one other demands of night navigation was their minimum convenient requirement, and they returned, coasting along the edge of the reef by the harbour and calling out until someone brought out a torch and tossed it aboard.

They set off for the second time then, and went right to the end of Tonga-tapu before David discovered that a chart he thought necessary was missing; and he turned again. This time they came opposite the village of Kolonga and swung to an anchor; but, after checking all the charts he had, David decided he could make do. They pulled up the anchor and, for the third time, set off.

This second return gave rise in after months to a rumour that they had returned to Kolonga to load a barrel of beer, or some other intoxicants to make a holiday of the voyage. But Tofa Ramsay, who with the responsibilities of ownership immediately investigated the story, says this is not true; they returned for the chart, and then decided they didn't need it.

With two false starts they were behind schedule; and when at last they cleared the island they found themselves headed into a vagrant wind, a wind from the south-south-west, coming straight to them from the port of Auckland, where they were headed. The date was 4th July; this is the heart of the south-east season, and they could have expected a south-easter that would boost them along on a beam reach—the regular trade wind of the South Pacific. Indeed, they could have expected it more easterly than that, so that the reach would have carried them exactly on their course. But the wind was just another unlucky factor, like the two omissions in their equipment, the torch and the chart.

The *Tuaikaepau* carried a twelve-gallon fuel tank, and on normal full power went about two hours to the gallon. She also carried a reserve of distillate of three forty-four gallon drums on this occasion; but without refuelling she could cruise for twenty-four hours.

Besides the wind, they were bucking a moderately high sea, and the landlubbers aboard were far from comfortable. Sipa Fine, indeed, in spite of a magnificent physique, was so sick that, not being apprised of the captain's intention to call at 'Ata, he believes today that his melancholy state was the reason for their visit. He had eaten nothing since leaving home, and he thought that in their kindness the crew proposed landing at 'Ata so that they could roast food for him.

They were not so considerate. And the state of the weather probably altered the courses of all their lives. For instead of making a dawn landfall at the island they came to it, after their late start and the headwind they encountered, at four in the afternoon; and David Fifita, in a mood that any frustrated navigator would understand, was ill-disposed to stay. They stayed, however; and the decision was significant. It was another factor that added up to establish the total tragedy, as well as the glory, of the Tongans of Minerva Reef.

Chapter Four

'ATA was an inhabited island once, chiming with human laughter, until, shortly after the year 1860, one of the twenty-five slavers that then operated out of Callao found it unprotected and made a savage raid, carrying off the pick of the able-bodied men to work in the nitrate fields of Chile. When news of the tragedy was brought to George Tupou he evacuated the rest of the island's population, finding them land and homes on the island of Eua, "The Garden of Tonga", where, eighty years later, the evacuees from erupting Niuafo'ou were also established.

Since that time 'Ata has had a great attraction for cruising Tongans. Its fishing is reported to be the best anywhere; the garden plants from its inhabited times still flourish; there are all kinds of riches on the island, and it is so far away that a special voyage is hardly worthwhile. Moreover, the island coasts are guarded by pinnacles of stone between which a dinghy or a canoe may be guided only with the greatest skill and care; and the waves create currents and swells which lead even the best of seamen to mistakes in judgment.

When *Tuaikaepau* let go her anchor a few hundred yards from the beach, most of the men got out their fishing-lines and began to fish. But five of them got into the dinghy and rowed ashore. Talo was in charge of the dinghy, Sipa Fine made sure he had a place because he needed solid ground to offset his incessant sea-sickness, and William Fa went because it was an adventure. Fatai Efiafi and one of the young boxers also went. It was a seven-foot dinghy; by European standards three men would have crowded it, but to Tongans, who are accustomed to rowing anything that rides, even fractionally, above the water, a five-man load seemed all right.

But as they tried to negotiate the pinnacles a big wave lifted them and threw them against the rock, staving in the boat and throwing them into the water. By David Fifita's orders they were all wearing their lifebelts; which was just as well, for not all of them were good swimmers. But they penetrated the channels between the rocks and came up safely enough on the beach.

With the careless resilience which is another character-istic of the Polynesian, they there proposed to carry on with their little expedition: to walk into the bush, to gather roots and fruits, to start a fire and cook their food. But David, angry at the mishap to the dinghy which he had seen from the cutter, shouted at them to come back. Seeing that they still hesitated, he sent his son Sateki swimming to the beach to see that his orders were obeyed. When Sateki arrived some of them, but not with a very good grace, entered the water and began to swim.

But some were frightened. The seas were increasing all the time, getting bigger and bigger, and the passage between the rocks seemed perilous. William Fa and Fatai were poor swimmers, each afraid to trust himself to the water. Of the others, some had found the lifebelts awkward for swimming, and discarded them. Sateki reached *Tuaikaepau* first; but seeing the situation he returned, swimming back with William and Fatai, one at a time; each time threading the dangerous wash from the rocks guarding the beach.

By that time the damaged dinghy had drifted far past *Tuaikaepau*, and Sateki set off after it, to secure it by the painter and drag it back to the ship's side. Even at that, his work was not done; for he returned to the beach to collect the lifebelts the swimmers had discarded, and swam back dragging them. He was a splendid swimmer, as completely at home in the water as on the land, and no normal task was beyond him.

The dinghy, lifted on deck, proved badly stove; it could be fixed, but the damage was so extensive that David decided it was a job for the boat-builder's yard. His carpenters, David Uaisele and William Fa, had the ability but not the materials.

" 'Ata" means "shadow" or "shade", or sometimes "twilight", and while the island itself could not be blamed for the bad luck that thus far had dogged the voyage, the joy was gone out of the *Tuaikaepau's* stay. Those who were not members of the regular crew kept on fishing with some scant success; but when all else was secure on deck and dark had closed in David ordered the anchor hove up, and they were on their way.

They continued to travel on the engine alone. The wind was still from dead ahead, blowing straight to them from Auckland, in the south-south-west, where they were headed. It was a lively breeze. They held it in their faces until six in the morning of 5th July, when they set the sails, brought the ship round close-hauled to the wind, and held her on a port tack. This left them heading almost due west, a course which David estimated would clear them from the Minerva Reefs, which they would thus leave to the north.

It is probable that he chose the port tack rather than the starboard (on which no hazard whatever was to be found in many days of sailing) because he felt that the next likely wind-change would be a backing to the south-east; besides which, any easting he made would have to be compensated for later; but the risk he took was a considerable one. Not only did the Minerva Reefs lie in the seas to which *Tuaikaepau* pointed her bow, but the set also was westerly. And the Minervas were the only danger points David had to take into consideration until, some days later, he would come to the Kermadecs, far to the south.

On the evening of 6th July some of their friends in Tonga felt a change of wind, and thought of the voyagers. The concern they felt was momentary, and was associated with comfort rather than with safety, for any thought of disaster was remote. The Tonga Radio, a recently constituted commercial station which is establishing a wide influence over Tonga, Fiji, Samoa, Niue, the Cook Islands, the Lau group, and even as far as the Gilbert and Ellice and the Tokelaus, was broadcasting a programme of Tongan songs. On the *Tuaikaepau* most of the crew were below decks, listening to these songs with a tiny transistor radio which was also part of the ship's navigational equipment. One or two had turned in, but most were responding to their loved melodies.

Johnny Lousi took the helm about this time. The wind had freshened to such an extent that *Tuaikaepau* was driving along at about seven knots; the sea had also risen, and they were knifing through a maelstrom of curling crests.

The moon was in its third quarter, and lay dead ahead in the western sky, and the brilliant shimmer it threw back from the tops of the white horses was blinding. The noise of passage joined with the amplified music to mask any sound presaging danger ahead.

Johnny was thirsty. He called to Talo Fifita, also on watch, to hold the wheel a few seconds while he went below for a glass of water. Talo took the wheel, watched Johnny's disappearing back through the open hatchway, and noted his father David standing there, ready to come on deck himself.

At that moment the *Tuaikaepau* struck the outer boundary of the South Minerva Reef. It was a glancing blow under the keel; a blow so timed and placed that most of the men, including the regular seafarers, thought that they had overridden a floating log. They did not dream there could be anything more.

But with the blow Talo cried "Reef", and David was on deck in a flash. As he came up, the *Tuaikaepau* struck for the second time; and now they were in the midst of the heavy break. With the second blow the cutter encountered a coral cleft in such a manner that her bow turned towards the north, and she canted over.

David immediately went below again; told every man to put on his lifebelt, to go on deck and forward to the mast, to hold on there, and on no account to act in any other way without a direct order. The *Tuaikaepau* lay piled up, listing heavily, yet in such a way that the racing seas left deck and companionway more or less dry, since it was her port side lifted high against them. The angle of the companionway was an awkward one, yet every man negotiated it without apparent panic, and they all went forward to the mast.

Fine Feuiaki, the engineer, was lying asleep by his engine, and the crash woke him. But he wasn't the last man on

57

deck. That place went to Sipa Fine, with his sea-sickness; he struggled into his life-jacket and went on deck and was the last man at the mast.

At this moment a comber heavier than the others threw the *Tuaikaepau* bodily more deeply and more firmly into the cleft in the coral, taking her bow still farther round to starboard and casting it up in the air, and sending her stern to port. Her list was now straightened, but she was immovably wedged, and from this moment took the full force of driving seas upon her stern.

Now the waves came hammering up the sloping deck to the bow, where all seventeen were clustered about the mast. Each wave swirled around their waists; Ve'etutu the mate fastened a line to make it easier for them to cling in place, and David called the roll. Every man answered; so far they had lost no lives. Here they waited; there was nothing to do but wait, while the moon on their port beam now eased down to the horizon, and the seas rose, with a rising tide and a rising wind.

David knew, as every seaman there knew, that the worst was yet to come. A rise of tide of three or four feet to the peak of the flood, due at midnight, would mean that the seas which now broke around their waists would break over their heads. And it was not possible that any wooden ship, however sound, would take the battering to which the *Tuaikaepau* was subjected, a battering which she was taking on her weakest parts: the hatch, the coamings, and the roof of the deckhouse.

To combat a little the thrust of the waves they took in the jib, working in frantic spasms between the rollers, and made a little protection of its canvas.

And they prayed: not the frantic unintelligible prayers of frightened men, but a prayer given intelligently and considerately in David's comforting voice, a prayer to which they all responded.

Some among them were deathly afraid. Teiapa'a Bloomfield thought, and continued to think through the whole course of that wild and frightening night, that his last day was upon him. He could see no hope of relief from this blasting sea that left no spot of land uncovered for hundreds of miles in any direction; he had no faith that the hull on which he stood would survive; he was in a panic that he was able to recognize as panic; his mind was filled with the knowledge that he could not swim, and with the remorse arising from remembrance of his sour farewell to his father.

And Teiapa'a was the first man overboard. The moon was just above the horizon, obscured at times by the racing waves, when a breaker bigger than any before threw him clear of the bows. He fell floundering in the sea, crying and gasping in an element as alien to him as to any underprivileged child from a big city; and was astonished to feel the solidity of the ground beneath his feet as the wave receded and left him in a mighty trough.

From the *Tuaikaepau* deck someone threw him a rope. He grasped it and was hauled aboard, frantic with fear. If he felt someone assisting him he did not know it.

For Ve'etutu had gone with the same wave. He was making one of the constant adjustments to rope and canvas that the situation of the packed crowd demanded when the wave came striking up the deck and someone shouted a warning. He turned to take a new hold and what cover he could, but the wave bellied out the canvas that was stretched behind him and sent him flying into the maelstrom. For him it was no new experience; eventually he came aboard himself, over the bowsprit.

Ve'etutu doesn't see the incident that way. His story is that the wave threw him overboard; that while he floated a second wave sent Teiapa'a over the side to join him; that when Teiapa'a found his feet he, Ve'etutu, was right behind him, and clasped him by the elbows and threw him

59

up on the bowsprit, whence Teiapa'a was assisted aboard, Ve'etutu following.

But discrepancies were all that could be expected from memories of that confusion and fear; that straining of muscles to hold to life, those momentary glimpses doused by the swirling chill of the next hurrying wave. The truth remains that both men went overboard, and by a miracle, or the grace of God and the quick-thinking of their fellows and the speed of their own reactions, they came back; and the captain, fathering his complement, could count them all safe.

Others went over from time to time. As the tide rose and the waves came less impeded by the coral beneath, five went over together; and were brought back, to hold again to the lifelines secured to the mast.

The moon set at midnight, when the tide was at its peak; and now the confusion of an almost utter darkness added to the terror of those who were dominated by it. Some time later, perhaps an hour, the ship split. They were telling time by the moon; in their knowledge was the fact that for a moon in the first quarter or the third the high tide came at midnight, when the moon would set.

The ship could not withstand the waves. In all probability her back had broken long before; and probably, too, a good deal of her bottom was ripped out of her; the men could not know. But with the sea coming directly from the stern, with her deck—the weakest part—taking each hammer-blow of water; with the coamings and the hatchway obstructing and defying the onrush, she split, and when she split she fell apart from stern to stem.

The mast, to which they were all committed, fell out of her, and into the sea ahead of them, and the captain roared his orders for them all to cling to it. One man at least could not hear them. Vaiangina Unga, the copra planter, holding on hard by the mast, fell into the chasm when it opened, and found himself caught by the trousers, under the water. He struggled and pulled; he leaned over against the tugging of the chancy currents to find what prisoned him, and found that the splintered timbers near the keel, jagged edges thrust together here and working like teeth, had a good hold of the cloth which, since he'd been a careful and a prudent man, was too stout to rip.

He struggled while, in panic for the air, he swallowed eight mouthfuls of the water; or so he says, and so he believes; though there are those who will reject the idea that any man could keep a tally such as that under such duress. But he was thinking, and thinking calmly enough to save his life. Having struggled unavailingly for a time, he straightened up and unfastened his belt, slipped his legs through the legs of his trousers, and came to the surface; and never saw his trousers any more.

Vaiangina then made his way to where the sixteen others clung to the thirty-eight foot mast sprung whole from its step at the keelson; and there they rested a little while, and again the captain checked on them and saw that they were all there. It was only a minute, he says, since the mast had broken away.

Some of them at this early stage had a strong faith in their captain, and this was more than likely their salvation. Even Ve'etutu, a man of the sea, had never been so close to death before. Once, on the *Taufale*, he had been washed overboard, and the unsteered ship went on, leaving him with thoughts of death. He had been sitting on a box steering with a rope; the weather had been rough, and when the rope, a light line only, broke near his hand, he had gone overboard, box and all.

But the size of the seas, the pitching of the ship had been such that two women passengers were sitting on deck though the night was far gone. They had been trying to sleep, their heads covered with cloth; in the commotion of

Ve'etutu's fall they lifted their heads, saw him go, and aroused the crew. The ship hove to a little distance away and the crew picked him up after he had been forty minutes in the water. That had been an ordeal, but it was small and insignificant compared with this.

Now, following David's orders, the seventeen men worked the mast over the reef where they lay, and floated it back into quieter water, manoeuvring it till it lay directly in line with where the *Tuaikaepau* had struck, straight down from windward. They held it across the wind in a place where sometimes their feet touched on the reef beneath them; the tide was going out now, and the spells in which they could stand were longer. They were about eighty yards back from the wreck; and David told them to watch for driftwood.

It was in his mind that the only rescue from this place would be by sea, and themselves the only rescuers. He determined that, though they stood shoulder-deep in water, they would build a raft on which to follow the wind blowing direct from them to Tonga; to do it they had to make use of whatever flotsam came from the breaking up of the *Tuaikaepau*.

First to drift by was the lid of the hatch. They secured it, and roped it to the mast; for at least they had plenty of line from standing and running rigging. They made it as secure as they could, and they waited.

Half an hour later the port side of the vessel came in one large piece. The diagonal construction more or less ensured that *Tuaikaepau* would not disintegrate into its component planks but break in sections; they secured this large piece to the mast.

An hour later, when their footing was more sure upon the knives of coral beneath them, a third piece worked itself loose from whatever bolts and fastenings had held it to the deadwoods jammed in the coral cleft, and came floating to them; and they negotiated these three pieces and the mast into a pattern that looked a little seamanlike. Then they knew they had the basis of a craft that might possibly carry them to safety.

When it was an entity, Ve'etutu dived below the waves and found holdings in the coral to which he could moor the construction; and throughout the rest of the night he stayed in the water, looking to the security of the raft. But the others, worn out by their exertions, climbed aboard the raft, cold and shivering, to wait for daylight.

Ve'etutu comes from a family that has long sea traditions. He was born at Ha'afeva, a small island containing about 300 people, an island that scarcely seems to lift above the high tide's surface, an island where everyone takes his sustenance from the offerings of the coral reef. Ve'etutu went to primary school there, and when he had qualified he went on to Tupou College in Nuku'alofa, but stayed for only a few months of secondary schooling. He was born on 25th July 1920.

As soon as his schooldays were finished he went straight to a life of working on ships; and in the army, though he had no civilian qualifications, he was appointed to a captaincy and became a Master of Army Boats in the Tongan Defence Forces. When the army was disbanded he went back to the sea, and in 1952 secured his Home Trade Master's Certificate. He commanded the *Taufale*, the *Aimoana*, the *Fetu'umoana* in turn, but in 1956 he shipped on the *Aoniu* as an able-bodied seaman to take advantage of an opportunity to go to New Zealand. He liked New Zealand very much; Auckland was as large a city as he could imagine, and he had a fine time there.

Like David Fifita, Ve'etutu married a Ha'apai girl, and they have a family of five children, of which the eldest, at the time of the shipwreck, was ten.

The reef itself had no terrors for him. And additionally he was buoyed up by a tremendous faith in David Fifita, a faith that was shared in much the same degree by the other seamen—David Uaisele, for example—and that in a different way was paralleled by the confidence Talo and Sateki had in their father.

These five, all Roman Catholics, were very sincere in their religion, too, following David's leadership. Their religion was to tie them together in an intimacy of strength, though David played no favourites; and among the others, Mormons and Methodists, were men as strong and sincere in religious belief.

The pre-dawn light filtered in upon these seventeen desperate men; an élite of sorts, and normally accoutred with the appurtenances of an élite, but now, in the uniforms of leisure adapted to the exigencies of disaster, clownish in their apparel.

Sipa Fine wore, and was glad he wore, an elaborate training jersey with a hood; it was his insignia of success in the ring, since Tonga no longer has championship belts for its heavyweight contests. Soakai had such a belt; it was beneath the ocean, and he was never again to see it. At the other end of the scale from Sipa was Vaiangina without his trousers. He was miserable and cold, but more miserable still were the youngsters, Teiapa'a, and Finau Laione, and Johnny Sikimeti. Sipa Fine, weakened by days of sea-sickness, was also in poor shape, and the older ones, Fatai and Soakai, were worn out.

The increasing light showed a wide half-moon of reef that went off into the distance, intersecting the far western horizon. It was studded, as reefs are always studded, with great blocks of dead coral thrown up by the storms, but at a distance of perhaps a mile, or a mile and a half, there was also a shape or a construction which they could not identify, and which looked alien in this sea-place.

They were busier now than ever. The tide had receded, and in an hour, at six-thirty, would be at a dead low; and everywhere amongst the rocks were items which they needed for their projected raft voyage; items mostly of food: the yams and taro and lily-stems that had been stored below decks on *Tuaikaepau*. These had to be gathered, and there was a time limit. Everything the men needed had to be collected before the rising tide floated their raft and made it possible for them to set off to Tonga, if the wind held, or to Fiji, if they made only a few miles to the north before it swung to become the customary south-easter.

There was some hope also that they might pick up essentials like navigating instruments when the water receded enough for them to investigate the grave of their ship.

At first it seemed that they were having some success. They found some items of clothing; such items were not returned to their original owners, but instead the men followed the rule of "finders, keepers". Perhaps this made them a little more avid in their search.

They found the transistor radio, but it was smashed and useless. They also recovered a small oil-drum of about ten gallons capacity. With other objects they put this on top of the raft for later attention.

Those who were seamen were essential for the task of strengthening and stabilizing the raft. Of the other active men, those who were used to reef could not be spared from their beach-combing responsibilities. But David Fifita, as well as his followers, was intrigued by the shape that dominated the reef at the distance of a mile and a half. He sent Vaiangina, who was fit and courageous, but who had no knowledge of reef, to investigate.

Those who have walked on coral reef will perhaps have some conception of the ordeal that Vaiangina faced, without trousers, without shoes, negotiating the coral. His task was made a little easier by reason of the shingle that became exposed with the tide at a low ebb; and the latter part of his journey was lightened by his lightening heart as he realized that the object of his attention was a ship, thrown up on her side on the highest part of the reef, and, to outward appearances, very largely intact.

She was a wooden ship, perhaps eighty feet long with a beam of twenty-four, and as he drew nearer he could see Japanese characters painted on her stern. She lay northwest of the *Tuaikaepau*, with her keel facing that ship and the normal weather, which was why she had not been more immediately recognizable. Vaiangina guessed her to be one of the Japanese fishing-boats which, in fleets under the suzerainty of a mother-ship, exploit the resources of most corners of the Central Pacific and are a familiar sight in Tongan waters.

She lay at an eighty-five degree angle on her starboard beam, and though this, up to an average height of about five feet, was rotted and eroded away by the regular soakage and drainage of the tides, and had suffered, besides, considerable initial damage when the ship had been first cast up, the remainder was in fair condition, with the portside compartments, now high in the air, offering living-quarters which, if they were not ideal, were infinitely preferable to the refuge represented by the raft.

Vaiangina made some initial explorations; but, conscious of the need for haste made obvious by the turning of the tide, he returned in a very short time to where his companions were still scouring the reef. His report was that the ship offered living-quarters that were above high water and could be closed to the weather; and David, rather than sail so ill-prepared upon such a raft as they had already contrived, or could finish before the high tide floated it off again, made an immediate decision to use this shelter, at least until they could sail with confidence.

Since time was important still, he sent the very young and the most elderly, Soakai and the boys, to rest in the wreck. Meantime the others continued their work of salvage, without much success.

They had to wait there, anyway, until the tide enabled them to float their raft; for, having been under the arduous necessity of making it, they had no intention, as yet, of abandoning it. Thirty-eight feet long, fifteen feet wide, perhaps; a triangular construction, it yet was all they owned, their only hope of life, and they guarded it well. They placed all the treasures they had retrieved on its surface, and little by little, as the incoming tide made it easier, they pushed the raft northward and westward to the Japanese wreck, David and his two sons and Ve'etutu, Vaiangina, Fatai and Soakai's son, Fetaiaki. It was after midday before they got there.

In all the time they had been in the water they had seen no big fish, nor anything to remind them that this alien element was a covert for enemies. But as soon as they got to the Japanese wreck they looked down and saw a big shark in the water. They baited a hook with a clam and dropped it over the side of the wreck, and it lured the shark. By mid-afternoon they were making a meal of it, with taro and yams boiled in sea-water; but there was nothing at all to drink.

Chapter Five

THE excitement of exploration had contained the first men to reach the wreck, and it excluded them from the rest they thought to seek. It was a nightmare palace that opened up to them, a palace in which locker doors opened down from the ceiling, the glass domes that protected electric light bulbs thrust upward from the floor, doors opened like trapdoors, top and bottom, and there were portholes above their heads, keeping out the sky. Stairways lay on their sides, ladders stretched out horizontally, uselessly connecting equal levels; the galley stove could never be used again because of the attitude it had assumed. There were bunks enough for all, but they depended from the ceiling or stood edgeways on the floor.

The lower part of the vessel was useless. The castaways gained access to the upper by climbing the smooth and almost perpendicular deck, taking footholds in what had been the bridge windows, scraping away the slime that had gathered over the months in all exposed places. They found a name connected with the wreck—*Number 10, Noshemi Maru, K 30*—but they never used it.

Within the wreck the pervasive smell of sea-wrack and iodine dominated everything. A blanket reeked of it; the very wood of the partitions, though they still held protective coats of varnish, was saturated. It was not a bad smell, not a symptom of decay; but it was alien and concentrated.

There seemed, at first, a great deal to be found, but when all was added together there was little indeed. Such items as were valuable had no currency in the world of the reef —there was a direction-finder and a depth-finder which made David's mouth water when he saw them later; but here they had no use, nor any power to activate them.

There was an MF/DF radio transmitter still in good order, its leads still running to the radio mast. Had it been capable of working it could have transmitted its messages back to Tonga, or to New Zealand for that matter; with it the Japanese captains had communicated over a thousand miles of ocean. But it was powered by a twenty-four volt battery as well as by the generator on the engines; the discoverers reluctantly admitted before very long that there was nothing they could do with it.

Its last message must have accomplished the rescue and evacuation of the Japanese crew; and the message was effective, for there were no personal possessions left at all. Each Japanese had left the reef with all that was of value to him; no tools remained in the engine-room; no cutlery in the galley.

Fishing-gear of all descriptions was still in its place: miles of tarred line still brand new, thousands of hooks. And disaster's interruption of a successful voyage was announced by the condition of the storage hatches, crammed with fish skeletons.

Four hundred gallons of oil they found were later to

prove useful in maintaining the fire. There were ten gallons of lubricating oil in a drum that they later used. In the paint locker were quantities of paint, but no brushes; when David arrived he took possession, on that first day, of some cans of paint, a coil of asbestos caulking material, and some putty; he had made no decisions, but he knew that soon he would be occupied with problems, not of survival, but of escape; and for this these materials had a possible value.

They found blocks and pulleys in quantity and in various sizes, but no compound blocks, all single. There were pots and pans, but only a few. In the captain's room was some navigational equipment, including some charts; but they were not in English. There was a compass, still efficient. In a medicine locker were a bottle of iodine, a bottle of mercurochrome, a bottle of undated penicillin, and a syringe. There were exercise books, some crammed with observations in Japanese. There were folders of transparent plastic designed to keep working papers clean and dry.

Inside the cabins the varnish was still preserved on such appointments as the loud-hailer amplifiers; indeed, the cabins were in good order, save that the doors had to be entered on hands and knees and the starboard walls, about five degrees off the horizontal, had to serve as floors.

Hope was now ascendant in the normally optimistic hearts of the men; they felt that this was a place they could stay until such time as a search-party reached them; and they had no doubt that, after three weeks or so, parties would be organized, at least in Tonga. In this they did not count on certain psychological factors; the great respect in which the captain's abilities were held was to stand in the way of an organized search.

Hope was further confirmed when Johnny Lousi, almost a chain smoker, and certainly the heaviest smoker of this crew, discovered a single live match wedged in a crack of what had been the floor of the captain's cabin. A little later he found an empty match-box.

They cleared a space for a permanent fire in a companionway below deck where there was ample ventilation and where the fire would have protection from any weather. They laid a metal sheet here, and propped it up to an approximate level. Then with a table-knife, the only knife found in the wreck, Johnny Lousi carefully cut a heap of fine shavings from a splintered lining-board of pine, and set them against a rag saturated with oil, and ventured to try the match. He was successful, and they had a fire; and fire was essential to their continued life.

At a later stage David Fifita found a box containing fifteen matches. Four of these matches he gave to Soakai, against the chance that some accident would deprive him of the rest; but he told Soakai to keep it secret, and himself did not divulge that he had this insurance against the fire going out. For he felt it would be a good discipline, and a necessary one, to have the fire watched every moment of the day; and he was already concerned with discipline; he realized the necessity of maintaining and enhancing his ability to command, and knew that without an effective leader they were all doomed.

Johnny Lousi also found a packet of musty Japanese cigarettes. He kept some, and gave seven to David; David smoked them over the next three days, appreciating them while he abhorred their flavour.

Perhaps the most frustrating discovery consisted of five large tubs of soy sauce, big wooden tubs bound with twisted cane, and each holding six or seven gallons of the sauce, with contents intact. The discovery was frustrating because practically all the men loved soy sauce; but they knew it would increase their thirst, and they had nothing whatever to drink.

Perhaps the most useful find was a large nail, a six-inch

spike with a chisel end. They put it aside, and later it was to perform near-miracles for them.

That first night they were exhausted. They had been thirty-six hours without sleep. In that time they had worked like slaves, and the emotional impact of death's proximity had drained at least some of them of all their strength. They set a guard for the fire because the flame was precious, and before they slept they held a prayer meeting, setting a pattern for the days to follow. The captain had already chosen a compartment for himself and the mate to occupy; it was a way of preserving the authority which now was vested in him by the weakest of reasons, for he was surrounded by independent men, some of them noted for their ability to establish a dominion over others by physical means.

To this compartment the Catholics repaired; and when they had performed their devotions they joined the others, the two Mormons and the nine Wesleyans; and all prayed together.

The prayer meeting itself was, as the captain realized, an establishment of discipline. He was sincere in his faith and prayed initially to establish that communication with his God in which he felt secure; but he was fully aware that, like the maintenance of the fire, the prayer meeting could perform other functions necessary to their survival.

The next morning, 8th July, was a Sunday, and most if not all of the castaways were moved to keep it sacred; but in their necessity of finding food they could not. Again they had their prayer meeting to start the day; the tide was low and still on the ebb; and as soon as they could, they set out on the reef to the site where they had been wrecked; and to their joy there was a little more for them to salvage: a few roots of taro in crevices in the reef, a few poor items of clothing, much battered by the sea. And a treasure: a hammer. They had by no means exhausted the possibilities of the reef when the rising tide drove them back again.

That is a simple statement; it does not convey the sense of panic one feels on a reef when one's sanctuary is at some little distance; a distance of more than a mile may take two hours to negotiate, and in that time the water might swirl in two or more feet deep, for the flood gains velocity as it develops. A man knee-deep in water finds himself struggling up to his waist before he reaches his destination; the predatory sharks come in with the flood, for that is their habit of sustenance; a misstep anywhere can send the man over his head, and the currents can be strong. The Tongans knew reef too well to give way to panic, or at least some of them did; but the complete isolation of South Minerva added to their sense of peril possibly imminent.

Back at the wreck, confined to the upper decks, they rested. The afternoon sun reached them, and they were warm and, in spite of their situation, relaxed. But thirst was paramount. David had told them, while they were on the reef, to eat raw oysters, and to eat their fish raw if they could, thus preserving its content of water. The younger ones discussed their situation; some of the more thoughtful, after their evening prayers, indulged in some useful self-analysis.

Sipa Fine, for example, knew that if he thought about his predicament very deeply he had a recurrence of the fear that had gripped him throughout the night of the wreck. But he was conscious also of the comfort he had in the presence of his fellows. He had, he said later, "a kind of safety-in-numbers feeling about the situation". And he had a great faith in David. A good Mormon, he resolved to turn more closely to his faith, and this resolution, too, gave him some comfort.

Teiapa'a Bloomfield, more worldly than Sipa Fine, was

73

making other resolutions; mainly that at the first opportunity he would learn to swim. It had taken him time to
recover from the very real panic to which he had sub-
mitted; the highest point of his fear had been when he fell
into the water and knew his helplessness. In the rising tide,
before he came aboard an hour or two before that noon,
he immersed himself in a pool where the water came up
to his shoulders and tried to take his feet off the bottom
and kick himself along. It provided a little comic interlude
for his fellows, most of whom could not remember having
learnt to swim, for they had come to it as naturally as they
had come to walking, and at a comparable period in life.

Ve'etutu Pahulu, the mate, reproached himself because
he had not come to this emergency with the physical
fitness he would have liked. He determined to put himself
through a regime that would restore his muscles to iron
hardness; he did not know what calls he would have to
make upon his strength, but he determined that his body
would be adequate to them. A religious man, he put his
faith in God; he had an enormous trust, too, in David
Fifita, but he was determined that his physique would be
adequate to any call made upon it.

Talo, Sateki, Fine Feuiaki the engineer, and Soakai were
inclined to put their faith in the captain. Soakai, for all his
years and experience, perhaps has less religious faith than
any of the others, but he did nothing and said nothing that
would disturb their beliefs.

"I had plenty of faith while I was on South Minerva,"
he has said since, "but my faith was in men rather than in
religion."

Vaiangina, on the other hand, had a faith in his own
destiny. From the first moment they had struck trouble he
had a conviction that, no matter what happened, no matter
how long they stayed on the reef, or how many died, he
would be one of the survivors. Though he knew nothing

74

of the sea he was not overawed. A Mormon, he has a strong religious bent.

About this time David appointed Ve'etutu, Vaiangina, and Soakai as lieutenants, and began to set tasks for the men. On this day, too, he contrived a small still for getting fresh water from the sea; it was inefficient, and the total daily supply gave them about an ounce and a half for each man twice a day. They measured it out in a Japanese *sake* glass with three Japanese characters etched in black into its surface; and morning and evening they lined up for this pittance.

Their day was ruled by the tide, which permitted them on the reef for a few hours only; but now they were organized into teams which filled in the remainder of their hours on the wreck with useful work. From the middle rail of the bulwarks they cut mild steel which they hammered into harpoons for fishing; more for protection from the sharks which, they knew now, cruised hungrily for ever up and down the outer boundaries of the reef and, as the tide rose, ranged the shallow water over its surface.

For these first days most of the time on the reef was occupied with reclamation of wreckage from *Tuaikaepau*, and at this period they concentrated upon the edible roots that washed up. But while they were confined to the Japanese wreck they began to paint distress messages on planks. They found a single small brush, intended for cleaning odd corners of machinery rather than for painting; they used this, and also their fingers, and scraps of half-rotted tarpaulin.

SOS 17 MEN ON MINEVER REEF APP 196 M SW OF ATA, they spelled out. They painted both sides of each board, primarily using the odd planks that were loose, and planks from the *Tuaikaepau*; though as yet they did not dismantle the *Vakavaka'amei*, the raft they had built; it remained moored alongside, above a small beach which had formed on the lagoon side of the wreck, opposite its tilted deck.

On the darker part of the beam of the Jap, where some traces of bottom paint yet remained, they carefully painted "SOS" in letters eight feet high, repeating the message so that the area it covered was nearly thirty feet long, and plainly visible to aircraft, even aircraft flying at great heights.

At all times now a gang watched the fire, night and day, distilling the water; and other men were told off to procure firewood. They were praying for rain; for anything that would relieve their growing distress; and each evening they carefully spread their best canvas, the staysail, the main, and the jib from the *Tuaikaepau*, to catch whatever drops might fall. But there was no rain.

As for food, they had no worries; not, at least, as to its bulk. They were still living on the roots they had recovered, supplemented with the fish they caught, and they had no trouble, and anticipated no trouble, catching fish. In every pool large specimens, never before disturbed by men, waited for the incoming tide, without the chance of a getaway. Clams were everywhere, and sea-urchins and oysters, with octopus and crayfish to be picked up by any agile hand, and eels to be speared.

The fish included rock-cod, parrot fish, schnapper and sharks, and the varieties that Tongans know as *monuafi*, *nue*, and *pone*.

But David, with a working knowledge of the dangers of scurvy and related deficiency diseases, was worried that there were no seaweeds on the reef. Seaweeds and corals seldom grow together; untrained observers are sometimes deceived by the fact that some corals are soft, and some anemones look like coral; and both may wave about in the water like weed. But seaweeds, if they had existed, could have supplied the Vitamin C in which the castaways' diet

76

was deficient. It could have been supplied, perhaps, by the algae which are found in conjunction with coral; but the men knew no way of making use of these. . . .

On this Monday evening, the evening of 9th July, the Americans at Johnston Island, 2,800 miles to the north-east, released their "rainbow bomb"; or, in a more official phraseology, "a rocket-borne nuclear device was exploded two hundred miles above Johnston Island in the Pacific". The "successful" explosion followed two failures in the month of June, and four twenty-four-hour postponements. The blast, equal to a million or more tons of trinitrotoluene, created a pink and red glow that tinted the clouds like a sunset, a glow that stayed in the clouds for seven minutes, that was the visible evidence of an extra-atmospheric commotion that blacked out communication throughout the Pacific for up to forty minutes, and that was seen from Hawaii to New Zealand.

Some trained observers disbelieved the altitude announced, and gave their own estimates instead. These ranged upward to 1,400 miles. The bomb was designed, publicity said, to test the effects of such explosions upon radar and radio communications; and certainly it interrupted them, as forecast.

Some spectacular visual effects were reported. The initial green flash turning pink and red produced awe in Hawaii; an artificial aurora following a red-to-crimson flash shot through with white lines impressed New Zealand; bands of green, blue, yellow and white light changing to orange and vivid crimson, an effect that lasted for five minutes, was noted in Fiji. From most points came reports of an aurora-like effect that remained for an hour.

It was the biggest fireball ever produced by anyone less than the Creator; for in the emptiness of space there was no air to contain it.

And on South Minerva, sitting disconsolate on the upper deck of their refuge, the castaways saw it all; they had a better view, from horizon to horizon, than anyone else upon this earth, and it might be imagined that they were terrified, that they felt, perhaps, that while they remained the rest of the world was coming to its premature end. They could have been excused for thinking that the flaring heavens presaged a holocaust.

But they thought nothing of the sort. They all were literate and well enough read; and they knew the Americans had proposed to set off another bomb. They watched in some awe the evidence of man's capacity to interfere with the elements on which he is nourished and the communications he has devised; they admired the colours and the effects; and no doubt they wished that from the vast armada of ships, the vast armies of men devoted to this experiment in destruction, some elements could have been diverted to make a search for them.

They were not to know that on the following night Telstar was launched at private expense, to foreshadow the greatest improvement in communications yet devised. To derive benefit from such communications individual man must be welded, in his habits and occasions, with the vast body of his fellows; no brilliance of invention can assist those who, by accident or design, are divorced from modern society.

Yet another enterprise, on a lesser scale, was under consideration at this time that might, with luck, have released the castaways from their imprisonment without an effort on their part. For *Life* magazine in New York, planning to shoot a colour portfolio for its Christmas feature, "The Seven Seas", had almost decided to photograph the isolated atoll of North Minerva, eighteen miles away. Cameraman Leonard McCombe was given the assignment, and proposed to be at that location between the beginning and the middle of July.

North Minerva is a beautiful subject for photography, a circle of reef flattened on its north-west side, the flat pierced by the entrance which permits the flow of the tides. The centre, with its sandy bottom, shines limpidly, beautifully blue to the airborne eye, and the great regularity of the coral masses, no less than the isolation of the reef, makes it a fit subject.

But the aircraft available for the flight from Tonga had disabilities for photography; there was a distinct weather risk, since the plane had to be chartered in advance, and the nearly four-mile diameter of the circle to be photographed involved another restriction on the operator. Cost would have ranged between £300 and £900 Fijian, according to the aircraft used. Reluctantly, the *Life* editors decided that a smaller and more conveniently located atoll would suit their purposes better.

This expedition would not necessarily have sighted South Minerva, though, since so short a distance separated the two atolls, it is likely that the charter might have been extended to take it in.

And had the charterers been the means of saving the lives of a shipload of seventeen men as yet not reported missing, that would have constituted a milestone in journalistic history; and profits from the resulting feature might have run into high figures.

But 9th July passed without the miracle, and the castaways continued to do what they could. Investigation of the wreck continued to turn up articles of one sort or another that could prove useful. The net-covered fishing-floats of the Japanese were there in quantity; they consisted of large hollow glass balls eighteen inches or so in diameter. The men knocked holes in the tops of several, so that if rain should come they could be used for water containers.

Also with the fishing-gear was a large supply of cut-down rubber boots. There were far more than enough pairs for the seventeen, and they came in a variety of sizes; only David Fifita and his deckhand Johnny Lousi were unable to secure a fit.

There were few drinking-glasses and no cups. David found a seven-ounce beer glass and the *sake* glass, and kept them both for measures; but the others, wishing to find something to drink their water ration from, or to preserve it for a while, used bottles, or unscrewed the useless lamp-protectors from the companionways and cabins; cylinders of glass six or eight inches long and ending in a dome.

On Tuesday, Saia Peni had spells of a fainting sickness and was excused from work. The reef was dry later in the day now; the main task of each day was to recover anything from the *Tuaikaepau's* wreck, and some yams and taro that had floated off to sea on the first night were showing up again. The flood stream of the tide came gently eastward and brought them in; a stronger current to the west began with the ebb; and, as the set generally was westerly, the planks they painted were sent off in this as soon as the ebb had developed sufficiently to allow them to be launched at a place where they went immediately off into the deep water of the lagoon. Some of the boys, frequently Talo, would wade out into the water and send them away.

The planks carried with them a great freight of hope. Each day seven or eight planks, sometimes more, were laboriously painted and set afloat; it seemed impossible that some of them should not attract attention, either by being seen from a fishing-boat or by being cast up on a beach.

David himself thought it too early for rescue. There was little hope that they would be reported missing before three weeks, and possibly not for some time after that. He felt sure, however, that one or other of his captain brothers—Tolati, the skipper of the landing-craft *Kao*, or Pita in his fishing-boat—would investigate the Minerva Reefs. His problem was to keep his crew together and safe for this indefinite period. He had not altogether abandoned the idea of using the raft; but the winds anyway were not favourable; had they set off on it, it was unlikely that they would see land until they came to the great Indonesian chain, thousands of miles to the west. Except by the sheerest fluke they could not hope for succour that way.

Saia's illness worried David, too. He was not sure that it was an illness; Saia Peni was not the most willing of his workers, and he could very well have been faking. Poking about the deserted engine-room, he came upon a thermometer; not a medical thermometer, and with its calibration marked in Japanese characters. He tested it in his own mouth, and to his delight he got a reading. He was not sure what it was, but he marked the place. For a check he tried it on another healthy man, and finally on Saia.

There was no variation; but all this proved was that Saia had no fever. He had to be given the benefit of the doubt as to his illness.

David's greater concern was to set up a more efficient still to get fresh water. The kettle and the can which produced their few drops daily were not adequate; but without tools and without materials the job seemed hopeless. David prayed about it; he took all his problems to his God, but for this one he could see no solution until, when the fishing parties set out, they discovered a large forty-four gallon drum bobbing about in the water at the edge of the reef. It had a few gallons of lubricating oil in it, which they took out to feed the fire. Then David turned it over to David Uaisele.

With his hammer and his spike Uaisele made a careful cut a few inches beneath the top of the drum, and discarded the piece. On the open-headed tank left he hammered out the inequalities his work had created, while some of the other men teased out an old Japanese blanket, one of the few found in the wreck, to make a wool grummet to fit the top edge. There were nails in plenty now, by the fire; Finau Laione was making a collection of them and had started a big box; and Uaisele searched amongst them for sizes suitable for nailing together a wooden lid for his drum, cutting the timber with the end of the big spike-nail he had, driving it nearly through the wood in a pattern and then breaking the plank through at last.

The lid, fitted into the wool grummet over the drum, was nearly airtight. In its centre, still using the spike and the hammer, Uaisele punched a hole to take some inch hose; for there was a large quantity of hoses of all sizes in the store-room. He used the chisel-end of the spike to begin the hole, and then its octagonal side as a reamer, until it was an exact fit for the plastic hose.

Now, in spite of their taste for it, they sacrificed two tubs of the soy sauce. The emptied tubs, cleaned out and filled with cold salt-water, were for coiling the hose into for the condensation process. One end of eighteen feet of hose was fitted into the hole in the wooden lid, the other was put over the spout of the large aluminium kettle they had saved from the *Tuaikaepau*.

The process took longer than the telling. Cutting the hole alone occupied David Uaisele for three hours, and while he was doing that no one else could help much. It was 12th July before the still was finished, since only one man could work at a time; it was 13th July before it delivered water.

They were still finding yams; but they were cooking only one meal a day. Those men who needed more to eat could save some part of their ration; they also had the same chance as anyone else to eat the raw fish and shellfish which were in plenty on the reef.

Chapter Six

THE still was a great success; it was installed where the original fire had been, on the wall of the iron house which was extended down between decks in the otherwise wooden vessel. When it was fired with the enthusiasm these thirsting men displayed it delivered water with great regularity; and that first day they had an issue of twenty-one ounces each; it was the first time they had been able to quench thirst for six days. But they had used a great quantity of fuel; David ordered that the fire be kept burning more quietly, and thereafter they did not have so much.

The knowledge of how to build a still was in the training David undertook to get his master's certificate; he did not think so much of the achievement; but there is no book of instructions that tells how to make a still from such inadequate materials, with so limited a kit of tools.

Now all of the men were looking to the future with some equanimity; and some were already expecting the rescue ship to come poking over the north-eastern horizon, beyond which Tonga lay.

This was the pattern of their days: they began with prayer, the two meetings, one in the captain's cabin, the other in the larger compartment where the others slept. At the end of the prayer meeting work was allocated. There was a distilling crew to be kept busy now, to watch the fire and watch the water, and, as the fresh drinking-water collected in the kettle, to take it glass by glass and put it in the storage of a broken fishing-float.

Fishing was the main task still; a job for everyone, but one in which Ve'etutu the mate quite obviously excelled. But fishing depended on the tide. If it was low early in the morning, fishing would begin immediately after prayers; if it was at noon or later, then they would start by getting firewood for the distilling plant by stripping the ship's planks. There were partitions where this was easy enough; but most of the planks, well fastened, resisted the normal efforts of a man with a small hammer; a concerted effort by three or four men was needed to get a single plank, and it sometimes took them upwards of an hour. Another concerted effort was necessary to reduce the planks to manageable sizes.

A way more easily negotiable than the one they had was needed for the climb up the steep slope of the deck; the removal of decking from the beams beneath solved this, but took many man-hours.

The other effort continued, of painting planks with distress signals and setting them adrift.

Teiapa'a learnt how to swim very quickly. Before long he was enjoying the experience; it was no longer an ordeal. He was beginning to enjoy the swift excursions over the reef with Ve'etutu or Soakai; Soakai was an old drinking companion of his, but Ve'etutu could teach him more.

With his mind fixed on his physical-fitness programme

the mate hurried over the reef as long as the waters would let him, always deliberately trying to be, as he said, "a live spark; always on the go". He ate freely of all the fish he caught—small octopuses, shellfish, sea-eggs. When he caught a big fish he knocked a hole in its skull with his harpoon, and put his lips to it and sucked, taking in the blood and the brains, and whatever liquid there might be. The thought of doing that would in normal circumstances have been disgusting to him; but it was a discipline, and he found that it also kept his mouth fresh and sweet.

"The taste wasn't too pleasant," he grinned, remembering, months later, "but it was like following an order. I didn't turn from any food—I ate shark raw. I ate crayfish. I even ate octopus raw—it was tough, but I could do it. I ate the first living thing I came to. I tried to tell the rest to do the same, to follow suit. When I left the reef I was the one man who was most fit. I was 208 pounds when I left Tonga, 177 when I got back from the reef."

On the 13th of July one of the men discovered, at the site of the *Tuaikaepau*, what was to become in after days their greatest treasure: a Tongan Bible. It had lost its covers, and every page had edges tattered, and some were missing altogether. The glue was gone from the binding, most of the threads were broken, and in fact it looked like a loose packet of sodden leaves, and no use for anything. But they treasured it, and took it to the Japanese wreck; and, a few at a time, they dried the pages until they could turn them easily. They put the Bible aside for use at their prayer meetings, so that from this time on there were Bible readings, as well as their loved hymns, and an address from one or other of the senior members of the group.

Always, over the whole period that he spent on the reef, David Fifita was haunted by the fear that others might question his authority, and he devoted a good deal of thought to the ways in which it might be upheld. He transmitted small orders, for example, through the mate in preference to issuing them himself, and used his lieutenants as much as was humanly possible to keep order.

He determined also to set an example that his men would respect. When they were short of food he would be the one to go without. When they were short of water his would be the smallest share. When there was something to lift of which the weight was too great for any of the others he would lift it. As much as he could, he would do the apparently impossible—not from nobility, as he protested afterwards, but in defence of authority.

He also knew the importance of never deceiving the men: he would make no promises he could not carry out; he would play no favourites. And he hoped to give them a spiritual leadership, though they were not united in their beliefs, and he wished to make no concessions in the matter of his own.

He knew the temptations they were under, for he suffered them himself. Fatai Efiafi, whose actions were beginning to look like those of an unstable man, was in charge of a bottle of mercurochrome. He drank it. The captain had put the bottle of undated penicillin in the charge of Vaiangina, the syringe in Talo's hands, separating the items deliberately. But he heard a rumour that Vaiangina was wondering what penicillin would taste like; he took the bottle from him and the syringe from Talo, and kept them both in the cabin with the water, which was now under the guard of himself and Ve'etutu.

On 17th July he smoked the last of the cigarettes Johnny Lousi had picked up on the Japanese wreck, having kept it for a long time. He wished for more, and sometimes thereafter, when he felt the strain a bit too much, he made rolls of paper from the scribbling-books they found, and pretended these were cigarettes, setting fire to their ends as though he enjoyed the smoke. He discovered that others were doing the same. And some of them were heating their rations of water, to pretend that it was tea.

Ve'etutu in his travels, scouring the reef for good fishing-pools, found he could travel about a mile and a half or, on days when the springs brought extreme low tides, maybe two miles in either direction before he was forced to hurry back. Within this area he found the remains of three shipwrecks. Not much was left of them; sometimes the remains consisted of a pair of anchors; but the circumstances in which they lay signified that they represented tragedy and not a fast slipping of cables by a boat moored in safety.

One such anchor was enormous, and very old, with a stock twelve feet or more in length and an obsolete and awkward design. Two other ships were represented, besides the anchors, by the rusty remains of engines and shafts; one of these had carried a cargo of rifle-butts. They were brass-bound and finished, but there were no signs of barrels; and this was so noticeable that Ve'etutu rejected the theory, held briefly, that electrolytic action (induced in a sea-water medium by the presence of copper in the butts, and iron in the barrels) had eaten away the less noble metal. Several of the butts lay about the reef; he took a couple back to the Japanese wreck, and they used them as sledge-hammers to dislodge planks and decking for the fire.

On 18th July they found one or two more yams, nearly spoiled by the sea. These, like the others, they boiled in sea-water; they found them bitter to the taste, and the excess of salt increased their thirst. These were the last yams they had.

Soakai Pulu had been suffering from constipation since 9th July. He continued to eat, but he suffered considerably at times, and his belly was distended.

David was issuing the water ration in the evenings alone

now; he had found that if he issued it at noon they were thirsty again by evening. Without a noon issue they stayed more content throughout the night.

But with the drinking of the water, after the hot day in the sun, they were struck cold and shivered violently as from an ague. They might have done better to have mixed their water issue with some of the salt-water; or to have drunk a mouthful of sea-water before the fresh; for this was probably a symptom of salt deficiency; but they were afraid, and with reason, to begin drinking sea-water. In this they showed more sense and more restraint than the captain and crew of the *Minerva* a century and a third before; and possibly a licence to taste the sea might have done more harm than good.

Another symptom, distressing indeed to a cleanly people like the Tongans, was that they could no longer exercise complete control over their bladders. When they wanted to urinate they could not wait; sometimes not long enough to open their trousers (for such as still had trousers); the urine flowed on the instant that the desire hit them. It distressed them, and the worry of it exercised their minds.

The distribution of water rations was not without its moments of tension. The men watched each measure with a jealous eye, and complained bitterly if they thought that one got a fraction more than the others. It is probable that already some of them were beginning to steal water from the common store. They were afterwards honest in their confessions; but when they saw an opportunity to steal water they could not restrain themselves.

"I could not argue with my throat," said Saia Peni, who was probably the most incorrigible of these malefactors. But not one could point an accusing finger at any of the others; for of those who survived the rigours and perils of South Minerva Reef, only the captain, David Fifita, was

88

innocent of this crime against his fellows. In all probability the same was true of those who died.

On 24th July it became obvious that serious trouble might develop. The young lads began to dodge the work they were set. On that day there was a very slight drizzle; and probably there should have been some water collected from the sail; but there was none.

David Uaisele questioned Sipa Fine about it, and Sipa, from guilt or from resentment, responded strongly. There was a heated argument. Soakai, who when Sipa was in health was possibly the only man who could have bested him, managed to pacify the two of them; but David Fifita realized that the fight was only a symptom of an earlier build-up of tension.

After prayers that night he held the group together while he talked to them; and for the first time he threatened them. He reminded them that all, whether they had paid passage money or not, had signed on as crew members under himself as captain. Their past disobediences he would forgive them, he said. But if there were any further infractions of his rules he would report them when he got back to Tonga, and they would be punished by the authorities. He publicly named Ve'etutu, Vaiangina, and Soakai as his lieutenants again; this time making it official.

That was a bad day, the 24th of July. The weather had deteriorated to such an extent that it was impossible to go out on the reef at all, and the enforced restriction induced restlessness. It was impossible to paint the distress messages on the boards; the castaways were caged within their crazy shelter.

Sleep did not refresh them. No matter how they lay there was the angle of the floor. They would settle down with their heads uphill, and gradually, throughout the night, their bodies would fold down towards their feet (which they had anchored against some resistance); their blood vessels would become constricted, and they would wake with cramps and pains. These processes were accelerated when, at high water and in storm, their refuge was rocked by the waves. It was difficult to get more sleep than an hour at a time. Hour after hour they lay awake; and, as though lying awake were not enough, they then had to listen to the conversations of young Finau Laione, who talked all the time in his sleep, and slept better than all the rest.

Finau in his dreams passed pleasant hours with members of his family, his father and mother, his brothers and sisters. He had no nightmares; sleep brought him pleasant company. He chattered away most of the time. And though his physical condition was not good, though he was the first to show signs of deterioration in his build, his manner was bright and full of life; there was not a man on Minerva Reef who did not conceive an affection for little Finau.

The biggest worry now was Fatai Efiafi, whose mind was beginning to wander under the strain, though of them all, one would have felt, he was suffering the least pressure. He was the only one, not a young lad, who had no dependants; perhaps this was what left him with less drive, less determination than his fellows. He had been the first to discover the hold with the Japanese fishing-floats, some of which the men used for bottles. He thought they were his by right, and he put them aside. Sometimes he would collect a whole one he regarded as his own property; collect, too, his life-jacket and put it on and, doggedly, quietly, determinedly, set out to swim the 300 miles to Tonga. They had to put a guard on him; not only that, but he had to be pacified as though he were a child.

Fine Feuiaki was normally the appointed watchman on the wreck. Since he was the engineer, it was reckoned to be his duty; and now he frequently combined it with the frustrating task of looking after Fatai. In some degree

Fatai was lucky. He was better looked after, and better fed than the rest.

The water ration had now settled down to about ten ounces a day, with fourteen for sick men, amongst whom Fatai always qualified. Saia Peni was doing his best to qualify too, and a good many of the others were intolerant of these tactics, attributing them to Fatai also. It is just possible they may have been right in both instances.

But on 26th July Vaiangina became sick, and there was very little doubt about it.

"He was the first man to become sick," Soakai remembers, ignoring Saia Peni and Fatai Efiafi.

Vaiangina's feet were constantly cold; and his companions heated sea-water to put in the glass containers to warm them.

They had very little food in these days, first because of the storm, and second because it became difficult or impossible to fish in the disturbed and muddy water when they could get out. But on 27th July they caught twenty-one crayfish and 120 fish, each averaging about a foot in length, and there was plenty for all.

David at this time was not satisfied with the effectiveness of the distress messages they were sending out. Instead he ordered more elaborate constructions made, each consisting of three planks forming a triangle. A T-shape joining the centre of the triangle to its sides held up a short mast, well stayed with the Japanese lines of which they had such a quantity. The mast supported a square of partially rotted tarpaulin, on which was painted a distress message, with another message on the planks. These triangular floats were difficult to build, but there was little doubt of their ability to attract attention at sea.

In all they made thirty of these constructions, and set each one adrift on the westerly current. David kept a tally of everything he felt worth noting; by the time they had finished sending distress signals they had launched messages on 281 planks as well as the triangles, and in addition on some drums and other forms of float. All the messages were clearly lettered and could be read at some distance.

The plenitude of food did nothing to stop the bickering and argument that now began more openly among the castaways. Soakai, impatient with Saia Peni for, as he thought, faking illness, took hold of him and shook him; others might have thought it more violent than a shaking, initiated as it was by temper or exasperation, and Saia cried. That was a last straw for the remainder of the crew, and Saia and Fatai were told to go and find another room, another place to sleep where they would not disturb everyone. This they did.

Saia, normally a rather merry-looking character, doesn't seem a man to carry resentment; on the other hand, he thinks today that his worst memory, after that of the hunger and thirst he suffered, is of the fairly constant antagonism shown him by Soakai; though he's the first to admit that he earned some of it.

Usually he shared a distilling watch with Talo Fifita, who liked him, but whose normally tolerant disposition was ruffled by Saia's amorality. Saia got into so much trouble stealing water that Talo begged him to break it down; Talo would steal the water himself, he offered, and dole it out to Saia in such a way that its loss would not be detected. But nevertheless Saia stole, every time Talo went to replenish the salt-water in the still, or to do anything else that took him from Saia's side. It seemed that he took every chance he had to do something wrong; then he would be suspected, then confess, then break into tears and take his punishment.

But Talo was inclined to take sides with Saia because of a growing dislike for Soakai. For all his upholding of David's laws and authority, Soakai was not above coming with the gift of a crayfish or something like that, to beg a little stolen water from the distilling crew. When Talo and Saia were on watch Saia would naturally refuse him, but Talo would give in, and ration out an illegal mouthful of water. In the end, though, he came round to Saia's side and refused it. For one thing, Soakai was constantly upbraiding him for having run the *Tuaikaepau* on the reef; and before they left South Minerva he was to blame Talo (by the same reasoning) for the death of his son Fetaiaki.

Soakai was a bit rough with Johnny Sikimeti too, Talo felt; a few times he hit him, and Soakai's punch, still carrying the effectiveness of the champion, was not to be belittled.

Soakai used to take his ration of water, put it in a bottle that had once held medicine, and cap it with a small rubber nipple off some engine part. He had pierced the nipple with a hole so small that when he put it to his mouth he had to suck hard to get the tiniest quantity into his mouth; and from time to time he would refresh himself this way. He felt that this helped him a good deal, that his ration lasted all the longer. On 28th July Finau Laione stole the bottle from him and drank its contents. Soakai reported to David.

Once again David brought them all together and called a halt to stealing. He meted out no punishment, but he threatened plenty. He said that those who disobeyed orders would go short on rations, both of food and water. He had plaited a whip by this time, from some rope ends, and he now produced it. It was an effective-looking instrument, and he promised to use it.

He had another reason for calling the meeting. Some arguments had been based upon ownership of the clothes that had been recovered from the *Tuaikaepau*. Each man had been keeping what he had found. Now David ordered that every man's original clothes had to be returned to him;

93

and trousers, blankets, sheets, and towels thereupon changed hands.

The next day Johnny Sikimeti stole Soakai's bottle. Soakai stood *in loco parentis* to Sikimeti, whom he thought a promising boxer. Instead of reporting him Soakai boxed his ears, fairly hard, and called him greedy and selfish. As Sikimeti's acting manager, trainer, and father confessor he felt he had the right to do so.

All the previous day, 28th July, there had been very dark clouds, threatening rain; but no rain had come. They had cleaned out the still and made it a little more efficient; they had taken six inches of salt from the bottom of the drum after chipping it down.

The 29th of July was a Sunday, and in the afternoon David Fifita, who had eyes keener than anyone else's, saw a faint smoke in the western distance. The reef was between them and the smoke. The ship was heading east, on which course it would keep the reef to southward; but it passed too far away for them to entertain any real hope that it would investigate their signals.

When they saw it, however, they built up the fire and sent up a lot of smoke. That night, and for a long time thereafter, they had two parties on watch instead of one. A party under Ve'etutu kept an all-night vigil lest another ship should go past the reef, while a party under Soakai looked after the distilling of water. Ve'etutu's party was prepared to light another signal fire on top of the deck, from which vantage the flame would show well out to sea; and for this purpose they kept a coil of tar-covered, tar-impregnated Japanese fishing-line at hand. It burnt well.

Such a line was the cause of yet another argument between young Johnny Sikimeti and Soakai Pulu. It was a flare-up over very little. Soakai asked Johnny to cut off some of the line to brighten up the fire; Johnny was unable to accomplish it and Soakai hit him.

It is at least probable that such petty displays of temper were signs of the deficiency diseases that now threatened the whole party. Fish is deficient in Vitamin C and Vitamin B1; and, while the full effects of this deficency were not yet demonstrated, some symptoms and signs were beginning to appear. Within a few days most of the party were to find swellings beneath their chins, round their ears and elsewhere. Similar oedemas affected their ankles; in particular Talo's; they swelled alarmingly at times and would stay swollen for days. The swellings would recede and come again; no pain was associated with them, and after a while the victims ignored them. With the distensions of the underbelly, they were probably the oedemas of beriberi, which locate themselves wherever flesh is pendent or carries weight.

About the fourth or fifth week most of the castaways began to break out in boils and skin eruptions. And in Soakai's case there was his constipation; by the end of July it had been established three weeks, and it surely had a bearing on his shortness of temper.

On 1st August Soakai admitted in his diary to being in some extremity of thirst himself; he wrote that he bribed Talo with a roast crayfish to give him half a glass, or about three ounces, of water. Talo gave it to him, he says; and a few hours later Saia Peni came creeping to his bedside with another half-glass that he and Talo had filched for him.

"No matter what the amount of water, no matter what the means of getting it, this water was life," Soakai wrote in his gratitude.

The Sunday before, that 29th of July when the distant ship left her plume of smoke to stir the men's anxieties, was the night of their first rain, a passing shower, a really light shower at four in the morning. They were all instantly awake. The captain yelled that no one was to go near the canvas they had spread to catch the water; that was ship's water, and they should all go elsewhere, find some small spout or drip, enlarge some natural catchment on the wreck and help themselves.

Most of them did so, using whatever they could find to catch or to direct the water. But in the midst of the controlled excitement David Uaisele saw the figure of a man near the edge of the spread canvas, and guessed that he was stealing water. He had a bowl which was a section of a Japanese float; and he had it already half full. David Uaisele yelled at the man. It was Fine Feuiaki. In rage at being discovered, and half mad with frustration, Fine dashed the bowl against the timbers and broke it, wasting the water. Uaisele rushed Fine, and a fight developed, but David Fifita had heard the commotion and came and stopped it immediately. He took Fine to his cabin and lectured him.

However, from that rain they gathered two large floats full of water. It did not increase their water ration, for a number of reasons. In the first place, the more alert had slaked their thirst in the rain. In the second, they wanted to save fuel; though they had to keep the fire burning they had to use more wood in the distillation of water than merely in keeping the fire alight; and wood was becoming difficult to get. The captain therefore decided that the rainwater should replace, rather than augment, the distilled water. He felt, moreover, that the water ration was another discipline; it was proving sufficient, and it did help to keep the men in order.

David and Ve'etutu stored the rainwater in the cabin where they slept, and between the two of them kept up a twenty-four-hour guard on the bottles. There was thus less opportunity for the boys to steal water than there had been when they were on distilling watch.

Fetaiaki developed pains in his head and his stomach; he had this ague with chills, and his father Soakai advised him to lie down. In a little while his headache increased. Tei-apa'a Bloomfield brought him a small ration of hot water, and went to David full of concern for his friend. Thereafter the water always had to be warmed for Fetaiaki when he was sick.

At the church service on 5th August David took as his text verses fourteen and fifteen of the fiftieth Psalm:

"Offer unto God thanksgiving; and pay thy vows unto the most High:

"And call upon me in the day of trouble: I will deliver thee, and thou shalt glorify me."

Even Soakai, who, when he goes to church—and his record is rather lower than the Tongan average—is a member of the Church of Tonga, said that it was a stimulating sermon. In the afternoon they had a talk on the way the Israelites survived in the desert. Following their Sunday custom, they did not work that day.

But that Sunday night Johnny Sikimeti and Finau Laione, the two youngest, were swift to transgress.

Whenever the water was distilled it was measured glass by glass into the storage bottle, and this was taken to David's cabin with a report on how much the bottle contained. On this night it had been delivered with a reported tally of twenty-one glasses; but at the later distribution, when it came to be measured out, there were only seventeen in it. Four seven-ounce glasses were missing.

So it was assumed that Johnny Sikimeti and Finau Laione had got an unfair share of the water, and investigation, which proved this, showed that their method had been particularly crafty. The leader of the distilling party was Johnny Lousi. The two boys armed themselves with rubber tubes, and while on duty they took care to sit between Lousi and the bottle as much as they could. They had the tubes inside their sleeves, running up the insides of their arms; and whenever Lousi's attention was distracted they leaned over to slip the finger-end of the tube in the water. With the other end in their mouths they sucked up a few quick swallows. They were not seen, and managed to get away with it until the count.

On the following day, Monday, 6th August, there was a slight drizzle; not much; but they managed to save thirty-eight glasses of water out of it; and they had two glasses each that day instead of one and a half. The sick people were given three glasses each. By that time Johnny Siki-meti was among them. The others were Fatai Efiafi, Soak-ai's son Fetaiaki Pulu, and Sipa Fine the boxer. Fatai's craziness was now well advanced. He refused to eat with the others; in fact, he spent all his time in his own little hideaway on the wreck.

Chapter Seven

LETTERS from Tongans in Auckland, New Zealand, commenting on the non-arrival of the *Tuaikaepau* had been arriving in Nuku'alofa; and about this time, Captain J. T. Sutherland, the Port Captain, sent for Tofa Ramsay and queried him on the load his ship had been carrying.

"I'm suspicious of this long delay," he said. "I'm afraid something might have happened to the boys."

Tofa had no worries at all. He said that the men might have stayed at 'Ata for a week or two, if the fishing had been good and they were enjoying themselves ashore. Then they could have stayed at Raoul Island, or anywhere else on the Kermadecs. It would not be unlike Fifita to do that, and he was certainly under no restriction about it. As to disaster, Tofa didn't think that possible.

Captain Sutherland was inclined, privately, to agree with him. He thought that an extended picnic was a very reasonable solution of the cutter's disappearance; nevertheless the ship, for whatever reason, was missing, and "Missing" he reported her.

By mid-month the *Fiji Times* and some New Zealand papers were reporting that she had been missing for more than a fortnight. The *Pacific Islands Monthly*, which pays close attention to the movements of small ships in the Pacific, carried a notice about her in its two subsequent issues.

Before this, on 30th July, the New Zealand police, apparently after being approached by friends of the crew, applied to the Royal New Zealand Air Force for assistance in locating the *Tuaikaepau*. The police application was received at 11.45 a.m.; within five minutes initial action was taken. A signal was dispatched to Fiji seeking confirmation of departure and a description of the vessel, and aircraft and ships were briefed immediately to keep a lookout.

The reply from Fiji carried the information that *Tuaikaepau's* previous voyage from Tonga to Auckland had taken nineteen days; in fact it had taken only thirteen. The Fiji message also stated that the yacht's owner said his crew intended fishing off 'Ata for an unspecified period. In the light of this message officers decided that no further action was warranted at that stage.

Two days later Fiji advised that, as further information from Tonga indicated that *Tuaikaepau* proposed spending only a few hours at 'Ata, an aircraft had been dispatched to search the island and its waters. That search yielded negative results.

It was then learned from an Auckland friend of Fifita's, a man who had been approached because he had previously commanded *Tuaikaepau*, that it was customary for the voyage to be made by way of the Kermadec Islands. Acting on this information, the R.N.Z.A.F. made a search of the Kermadecs. Two aircraft, a Sunderland flying-boat and a Bristol Freighter from the Transport Support Unit based on Whenuapai, were sent out. They made intensive searches of the Kermadec group, concentrating on sea areas adjacent to Esperance Rock, Curtis Island, Macauley Island, and Raoul, sometimes called Sunday Island; they also conducted a square search over a significant portion of the sea between the Kermadecs and the port of Auckland.

The Sunderland made two sorties, with a total search time of fifteen hours, twenty-one minutes; the Bristol Freighter four sorties, with a total of thirty-two hours, eighteen minutes. The cost of this search amounted to £4,550 sterling. On the evening of 4th August deteriorating weather and a lack of any definite information on *Tuai-kaepau's* movements after its departure from Tonga persuaded the authorities of the futility of continuing the search. In fact it had been an efficient and smart operation, carried out with a minimum of delay. But sadly enough, the Minerva Reefs, representing the only other hazard on the Tonga-Auckland route, were not included because of a chain of unfortunate accidents.

For a start, the long delay before *Tuaikaepau* was reported missing, twenty-six days after her departure, led to a supposition that she had covered a good deal of her journey. Since rough weather had been reported round the Kermadecs at about the time *Tuaikaepau* might have been expected to get there, the search concentrated on this area.

The R.N.Z.A.F. maintains, at Lauthala Bay in Fiji, a flying-boat squadron with a Sunderland; the flying-boat which investigated 'Ata, and through which the New Zealand stations obtained their information. Had the Lauthala Bay search been continued past the investigation of 'Ata, their next target must surely have been the two Minerva Reefs.

But in any Air Force station the three functions of the

service—Operations, Training, and Search and Rescue—must each be allotted a due proportion of flying time. Flying-boats, amongst the islands of the Pacific, are more in demand than any other vehicles for so-called "mercy" flights. A man suddenly stricken with appendicitis on an island that is in any way remote must have his needs served; and the result is that Operations and Training tend to get less flying time than their requirement, particularly in Fiji with its 340 islands and its overseer function for the neighbouring groups of Tonga and Samoa.

To have continued an extensive search from Fiji would have meant the partial or temporary abandonment of some operational flying on which the station was then engaged; and station officers shared the fairly general conviction that a search in that quarter would have been a wild-goose chase anyway. Whether any other reasons were adjoined to the decision not to search the Minervas is difficult to say; the fact remains that this major hazard on the Tonga-New Zealand route was never looked at.

Sunia Bloomfield, the father of Teiapa'a, was anxious to have a search instituted; not of the Minervas, but of 'Ata and elsewhere. He was willing to pay some or all of the cost, but the price quoted him was well beyond his means.

David Fifita, a practical man, was conscious of the fact that, until mid-August, the chances of a search discovering them on the reef were better with every passing day; from that time on, however, they diminished rapidly.

From mid-July he had canvassed in his own mind the practicability of building a boat; he had decided that they would take this course, but felt that the time was not yet ripe. It would be impossible to build a craft capable of taking them all; and if some were to leave the reef the chances were that they would sail to disaster, and in the meantime a rescue party might save the others. Again it would involve a divided command; he could not be sure that the men were yet disciplined sufficiently in the interests of their own safety.

He also retained his faith that one or other of his brothers or both of them would come to look for him. He thought that the only reason they had not already appeared was that they were probably waiting for a government search to be instituted.

It was in this week that Finau Laione, the youngest of the party, stole a fish that had been set aside as bait for shark-fishing. Sharks were always cruising along the sides of the wreck at high tide; and David particularly wanted them caught for reasons subsequently demonstrated. Except when there was a surplus of fish, bait was a problem.

No one would admit to the theft, and, as in other cases of this nature, David held the men together after the normal prayer meeting. He said, "We are here now. We are in the hands of God. As far as the thief is concerned, it's quite possible he might get away with it here, but God may intercede. He might even decide upon punishment, and the guilty man may drown or be eaten by a fish. We all of us will have to account for all that we have done."

In the evening Finau came to Soakai:

"Please tell David it was I who stole the fish."

That night, the 9th of August, the storm arose. It was so rough that the Japanese wreck was rolling heavily in the surf that poured over the reef; it was rolling and groaning and bumping; making such a noise that the landlubbers feared for their lives.

At two in the morning the captain heard a cry, "Awake! Awake!" He got up to find the men all awake, all sitting up and oppressed by fear. Soakai Pulu had woken all who were asleep, and now, though he was the least religious of them all, he asked that all of them should pray together.

Fatai Efiafi, who at the moment seemed as rational, as

level-headed as he had been at the time of embarkation, begged leave to give the prayer.

He prayed long and earnestly, and they were all whole-heartedly with him; but nearing the end of his prayer he said:

"It is You Who rules the world, the waves and the weather. And if it is Thy divine wish that we should live to return to Tonga and our own beloved homes, then we thank Thee. But if it is Thy wish that we should die upon this reef, then Thy will be done."

At this Soakai interrupted, calling out, "No, No."

They looked up, startled, and Soakai said, "Let us take that back. Let us thank the Lord if He should return us to our homes, but let us not accept a condemnation to a death upon this reef."

"So each man got his wish," the captain said long afterwards. "For Soakai returned to Tonga, but Fatai died upon the reef."

On the next night, which was Friday, they caught four good sharks. On David's instructions they removed the long fawn-grey livers and sliced these into three-inch squares; there were fifty-six such portions. Constipation had been troubling most of the crew, and on David's orders they each ate, raw, three of the squares of liver, warm as they came from the shark. But Soakai, who had been constipated for thirty-two days, since the night of 9th July, had to eat eight of the squares. He did so, and the rough cure was effective.

"I was very glad when it worked," Soakai remembers.

Another fish was stolen that night; and the bad feeling between Soakai and some of the lads came out into the open. He had an argument with Sipa Fine; and in the course of it Sipa revealed that it was he who had stolen the fish and eaten it. The upshot of that was that David called Soakai aside, and told him not to be too harsh with the boys; to temper his discipline with a little forgiveness and, above all, not to use his fists on them.

The weather cleared, and they had an abundance of food. They were getting sixty or more crayfish every day now, diving in the pools around the reef for them. They were amazed by the quantities available there.

On that Sunday they fasted, by David's orders. Ve'etutu took the morning session, and David the one in the afternoon. They had food: crayfish and clams, left over from the previous day, but they were not allowed to eat them. For his afternoon text David read the first chapter of the Book of Job:

"There was a man in the land of Uz, whose name was Job; and that man was perfect and upright, and one that feared God, and eschewed evil. . . ."

He read the story, one of the greatest literary works the world has known, in the beautiful liquid Tongan words: how Job prospered, and was rich in sons and daughters, in flocks and herds and a very great household; how Satan, talking to the Lord, related Job's uprightness to his prosperity. . . . "But put forth thine hand now, and touch all that he hath, and he will curse thee to thy face.

"And the Lord said unto Satan, Behold, all that he hath is in thy power; only upon himself put not forth thine hand."

And Job's sons and daughters were slain, his herds were driven off, his servants killed, and his house destroyed.

"Then Job arose, and rent his mantle, and shaved his head, and fell down upon the ground, and worshipped.

"And said, Naked came I out of my mother's womb, and naked shall I return thither: the Lord gave, and the Lord hath taken away; blessed be the name of the Lord.

"In all this Job sinned not, nor charged God foolishly."

The Tongans on the Japanese wreck waited throughout the remainder of the afternoon, and in the evening David took the service once again. He began by reading from the Psalms, some of his favourites. Then he spoke, but briefly. He said:

"What is each person here going to do when he gets back to Tonga to show that he is for Christ? What will he do to show that he appreciates the guidance of God? Remember the seventh of July, and remember it always. And each year when it comes again, think hard. Remember your cry to God for help on Minerva Reef on this seventh of July when we wrecked our ship. Always keep that cry in mind, and your request in mind, when you are back in Tonga, in safety."

Soakai, non-Churchman though he was and is, added the benediction.

After that, for the first time that day, they broke their fast.

This was good religion, but it was also wonderful psychology. The timing of these admonitions, the extra weight given them by the period of fasting, could not have been bettered.

Soakai had a dream that night, and in his dream a telegram came to him from David's younger brother to say that the *Hifofua* was to go to Minerva Reef, because the *Kao* had gone aground there. David Fifita, captain of the *Kao*, was stranded there with seventeen crew members.

It was the first of Soakai's dreams on the reef, and it was a short dream. He didn't even have time to sign the white receipt for the chocolate-brown telegram (always presented together by the Tongan telegraph boy) before he woke up. But he took it to be a good omen, and he told his son Fetaiaki, who was awake, that they were going to be rescued soon. In fact, the dream impressed him so much that he went up to tell the watch at the fire. He says now that the yarn must have inspired them; he frequently told them stories, mainly the stories of films he had seen, but this was his first dream. They managed to distil thirty-six glasses of water. The next day they caught 150 crayfish. But perhaps the credit should go to David's day of deep reflection.

They were beginning to dream a lot at this time, and Soakai's dreams were always of survival. One night, for example, he dreamed he was at a kava party in Tonga. Another time he envisaged a boat's crew coming to the reef where they were, and taking them off. Still another time he found himself at the Post Office in Tonga, talking to a clerk he knew well. He said to him that when they began looking for the *Tuaikaepau* they should try first at the Minerva Reefs. He left the clerk and met the Minister of Police, and by this time he was beginning to feel a little indignant. He said to the minister too, "Why don't you start searching for the *Tuaikaepau* men? And when you start why don't you try the Minerva Reefs?" He went on down the road without waiting for a reply, and met people singing, and a few girls doing the hula. His son was with him, so he said, "Give me a clean shirt to wear." His intention was to go back and tell one of the other cabinet ministers that the people were dancing and singing, and taking no notice, while the *Tuaikaepau* men were lost; but at this stage he woke up.

They had their first relief from an all-fish diet at this mid-August when Sipa Fine, walking down the reef, saw a mollyhawk sitting on a pool in his path. As he came up it flew awkwardly away, but it alighted again, a little distance from him. He approached again, and this time it remained, so that he caught it with his hands.

He brought it back to the ship alive, and they tied it up for the night; but in the morning it was dead, and they roasted it for that day's meal. Sipa Fine, after the bird had been roasted, asked for special prayers. He believed that in some way the catching of the bird was an omen, and that rescue was at hand.

Talo and Saia Peni had a fight, and Saia went to David, full of his own unhappiness. Among other things, he asked for his next day's ration of food and water in advance. He was at his most persuasive, but David, of course, would not give in. Saia then gave way to fainting spells, but these elicited no sympathy.

Next day William Fa reported a fish stolen from his ration. Sipa Fine told Soakai that there had been some doubt over the ownership of the fish; that Saia, who had owned it in the first place, had given it to William for some consideration and then taken it back. Soakai reported the matter to David. On the following day, a Sunday, after the morning service, David asked for the man who had taken the fish to give himself up. This time he sounded less reasonable than on previous occasions; he swung the whip he had made, and looked like using it.

Saia got up and confessed to stealing the fish, and additionally to stealing water that had not been mentioned as missing; for he had a fairly shrewd idea that his guilt was known anyway. David told Saia to ask God for strength to keep him honest. A little while later, meeting Soakai, Saia cursed him for incriminating him; Soakai seized him by the throat and hit him hard. As a result he too came in for a verbal drubbing from the captain, rather more severe than Saia's.

In the middle of that day, from 9 a.m. to 3 p.m., there was a slight drizzle, and from the spread sails they collected two big bottles of rainwater. Soakai, like most of the others, found a spot where he could divert drainage to collect it for himself; and with this drizzle his contrivances were particularly effective. He drank too much and was sick, and felt cold; unnaturally cold and shivering as with an ague.

Next day he had a bath of hot sea-water, using, as they all did, one of the empty soy-sauce tubs. Saia got to it first, and smeared it with heavy oil, which Soakai couldn't see against the darkness of the soy-stained tub and in the dim light between decks. Instead he climbed right in and came out a greasy black mess. It took him days to clean it off.

This was the period in which the internal dangers threatening the company on the reef rose to a high peak. Everyone was nervous and edgy; each was suspicious of the others. All of them knew that everyone, as his chance came, stole, either preferred fish or water; and though the amounts this disposed of were small the importance of any theft loomed large.

There were plenty of fish, though their hours for catching them were so limited. On their best day they brought in 335; but still the choice varieties were stolen. The men fishing would come in with their catch and secrete a fish or two in a pool near the wreck, or smuggle one aboard instead of adding it to the common store.

Vaiangina and Sipa, for example, secreted two big fish one day, delivered up the small ones they had caught, and at the first appropriate moment got out of sight to eat their concealed prizes—and Vaiangina was looked upon as one of the most responsible of the men. David found out, and repeated his order that all fish had to be brought in. He got so tough that Vaiangina started to cry, for fear that he had lost David's trust and confidence, and to ask forgiveness. Soakai sought out Vaiangina over this, and told him not to run with the younger crowd.

"You will split the command," he warned him. "You'll weaken David's position."

The Wednesday of that week was a very rough day, and they were confined to the wreck, except at some hazard. David instituted a rescue drill; a rehearsal of what would happen when the rescuing ship arrived. He called it a "last moments" drill; and it was a desperate attempt to engage the attention of the men, to offset the spreading disease of discontent.

The drill began with prayer, and during this prayer the Tongan flag was raised to the masthead. After the service the flag was lowered, and each person collected his belongings and the mementoes he proposed to take back home, and lined up to march to the rescue boat. No one was to take more than he could carry. At the landing-place, where they pretended the boat had arrived for them, there was another short prayer; then they were told that at this stage they would listen to the orders that would undoubtedly be given them by the officer in charge of the boat, concerning the next procedures. At the first sight of the coast of Tonga, on their return, there was to be still another prayer in which they would thank God for a safe return to their homeland.

Since it was so rough a day, David ordered then that each person should secure his own food. If anyone thought he could get out and catch a fish he was welcome to try.

Most of them attended to small domestic duties like mending clothes. They wore what they could, for they felt the cold, but the rough wear had reduced most things to ribbons. They mended them by using small pieces of wire as awls, and drawing through the better threads of the warp of tarpaulins.

Saia Peni, on watch that night, fell asleep and let the main fire go out. That was the first time it had gone out since they lit it. Luckily, because it had been so cold, some of the lads had taken another small fire to their sleeping-quarters.

Soakai, finding the sleeping lad and the cold fire, sent Saia Peni to David, while he investigated this other fire. One small ember was still red, an ember no larger than a cigarette end. Soakai woke Fetaiaki and told him to get the fire going, giving him some threads of wool. Fetaiaki managed to get the ember into a small fire, laying the wool and some splinters against it and blowing gently; and he kept that alight until daylight.

Next day David called a council and told everyone of Saia's neglect, not that they didn't know already through the whispers. It did nothing for Saia's popularity; but in a way it was good for the men on the reef to have a villain; particularly a villain with a certain engaging charm like Saia. It cemented the rest together; it gave them a scapegoat. Though they had all offended against the laws of Minerva Reef, they all could salve their consciences by pointing to someone worse than themselves.

They had improved the water supply by cutting the hose that formed the condensation coils. By reducing it to a third of its original length they formed a more efficient still, and regular cleaning of the salt from the drum kept it producing a good supply.

About this time the captain found a bag of rice on the wreck. It was in the rope storage hold, a compartment which they entered through an opening under the stern of the ship where the planks had broken away on the starboard, or underneath side. Though they believed they had combed the ship thoroughly, no one had discovered the rice before, because it was covered with coils of old rope which, since it was unprotected by tar and partially exposed to weather and to an occasional soaking with seawater, had gone rotten.

The captain was thinking of tools; it had become urgent and essential to find tools for boat-building, because he was fast losing faith that any rescue would come, save of their own efforts. He entered this hold with some difficulty, and when he lifted the top coils of rope they fell apart in his hands. He removed this hempen rubbish, and dug down.

To his amazement his hands discovered the shape of a filled rice-bag.

The grain had been packed in a double bag, with sacking outside and reed matting within. Both these materials were so rotted that the least touch crumbled them away, but the rice held firm in sack shape. It was black and rotten; but at least it was grain. It provided an element the captain had to think over; one of the difficulties of command was that he had no rewards for good service. This rice could constitute a reward for some arduous duties he had in mind for the men. He covered it up with rope, more or less as he had found it, and went away. Since the tide had come in while he was investigating, and since the usable entrance to this hold was from underneath, he had, in any case, to leave it for another day; and in the meantime he could think about it.

He told Ve'etutu about it. He said that, in the morning, the two of them would carry the rice to his cabin. He estimated that it had been a seventy-pound bag. Once it was safe in the cabin he would supervise the sharing of it on appropriate occasions.

The information that rice had been found leaked out, and during the night Saia Peni, Teiapa'a Bloomfield, and Johnny Lousi went down and found the sorry-looking treasure. They tied small portions of it tightly in squares of canvas and boiled these in the sea-water of the still, as though they were puddings in their bags. They took the rice out after a reasonable cooking time, and ate it; and later on they were to confess that, cooked by that method, it wasn't salty at all.

Soakai Pulu was on watch, and couldn't understand why the three men didn't want to leave the fire that night and get their normal sleep. He pretended to go off on some errand that would take him a while, came back, and to his amazement found that they were eating rice. Ve'etutu Pahulu then joined him, and was apparently as indignant as Soakai about the theft, and reported them.

But David Fifita had his wits about him. How could they have known of the rice, he asked, if Ve'etutu himself weren't in the scheme with them? The only person David had told was Ve'etutu, and it must have been through him that the intelligence leaked out.

So once again the culprits escaped a punishment.

They brought the remainder of the rice from the rope-hold to the captain's cabin, and there discovered it was so weathered and friable that when rubbed between the palms of the hands it would disintegrate into a flour. Teams of men were put on the task, the grain was rubbed into flour, and the flour stored in one of the soya-sauce tubs in the captain's cabin.

They would eat the rice, David told them, but only on days when there was a surplus of water and they had worked well. At the same time they would have to be successful in their fishing. Then the fish would be cooked all together, and made into a broth with the addition of a little water. Two or three cupfuls of the flour would be used to thicken the broth.

This is more or less the basis of a Tongan dish called "kiki"; a very economical way of spreading the contents of a two-shilling tin of sardines, for instance, amongst a family of six; an important point in Tonga, the only country in the world where labour laws dictate the maximum and neglect to state the minimum wage payable for any job.

After meals of this familiar food the men felt much stronger and more heartened. In the remainder of their stay on the reef they were to have twelve such meals; always on days when a lot of hard work had been done. The social atmosphere was all the better for them.

But in the incident of the theft there was a great danger that the ranks would be split with resentments and accusations. There was some muttering and discontent. So David attacked the matter directly, called a council meeting next morning, and told the rest of the people how and by whom the rice had been stolen.

Two days later, though, on Thursday night, 23rd August, Saia got into trouble. He was on distilling duty and had failed to collect his firewood. David penalized him by giving him no water ration at all for that day. As there was no fishing he had nothing to eat either. This was the first actual punishment inflicted on Minerva Reef.

Next day Ve'etutu reported that the night before he had caught Saia eating rice. It seemed impossible, but it was true, as Saia himself confessed. The night he had gone with Teiapa'a Bloomfield and Johnny Lousi to steal the rice he had concealed a further amount even from his companions in crime; and at this first opportunity he had been having a good meal.

Not too much was done about this at the time, for Friday was David Uaisele's birthday. Except for the first birthday, this is not a great occasion in Tonga, but a Tongan usually likes to have a special meal, a few bottles of beer, or whatever he can arrange to mark the day. The weather relented, they caught great quantities of crayfish, and had a special little birthday party with crayfish boiled and roasted.

On Sunday David preached the story of Elijah, from the First Book of Kings, chapter seventeen:

"And when he had come to the gate of the city, behold, the widow woman was there gathering of sticks: and he called to her, and said, Fetch me, I pray thee, a little water in a vessel, that I may drink.

"And as she was going to fetch it, he called to her, and said, Bring me, I pray thee, a morsel of bread in thine hand.

"And she said, As the Lord thy God liveth, I have not

114

a cake, but an handful of meal in a barrel, and a little oil in a cruse: and, behold, I am gathering two sticks, that I may go in and dress it for me and my son, that we may eat it, and die.

"And Elijah said unto her, Fear not; go and do as thou hast said: but make me thereof a little cake first, and bring it unto me, and after make for thee and for thy son.

"For thus saith the Lord God of Israel, The barrel of meal shall not waste, neither shall the cruse of oil fail, until the day that the Lord sendeth rain upon the earth.

"And she went and did according to the saying of Elijah: and she, and he, and her house, did eat many days.

"And the barrel of meal wasted not, neither did the cruse of oil fail, according to the word of the Lord, which he spake by Elijah."

Ve'etutu, whose mind worked more directly, took the service in the afternoon. He preached on the wrath of God engendered when people stole the offerings from the temples; the impatience of God with thieves.

Chapter Eight

THE chances of rescue receded with increasing speed, and were soon remote; and David's worries were augmented by the knowledge that this was in everyone's consciousness as in his own. It had become mandatory for them to make a successful effort to cross the wide ocean; it was a nightmare of David's that some of his crew, young, adventurous, courageous as they were, would make the effort without his knowledge or consent.

Twice Sipa Fine came to him and asked that he be allowed to set off on a raft—Sipa Fine, to whom a comfortable cabin on a seaworthy schooner represented torture.

"All very well," said David. "But what if, just when you have gone, some help arrives for the rest of us?"

That pacified Sipa, but there were others who thought the same way, who might make a more knowledgeable voyage on whatever was available. The *Vakavaka'amei*, the raft they had contrived from the break-up of *Tuai-*

kaepau, still floated near the Japanese wreck. On a day towards the end of August David gave orders to set about repairs to it.

This was an excitement; but there were other tasks: the water to be distilled, the firewood to be wrenched, splinter by splinter, from the reluctantly yielding Japanese hulk, the fish to be caught, the sick to be administered to.

William Fa and Fine Feuiaki went fishing; the carpenter on holiday, and the engineer-watchman. They were moderately successful; they caught a few fish each, good big ones; and, besides, they secured a number of crayfish from the crannies of the reef pools. It was impossible, at least for them in their weakened state, to carry their catch back home. They waited till the tide came running in, and then, their loads threaded on a line, began to tow them through the water back to their home, the wreck. They kept an eye out for sharks; sharks frequently followed the towed fish, and their menace was sufficient to make the fishermen wary as to the path they took.

But these two had hardly started when Fine Feuiaki cried out loud and collapsed in the water. His knees had given under him; he was attacked by cramps so virulent he could no longer control his muscles; and he called to William Fa for help.

William was dragging his two big fish and carrying seven crayfish and a steel harpoon. The fishing parties always carried the harpoon; sometimes it secured them a fish; sometimes it was a defence against the sharks; but on the latter David had warned them not to use it unless they were sure of hitting a vital point. A wounded shark could put up a good fight; he could do some damage. Besides, they could not afford to lose the harpoon.

William came back to Fine and asked him what was the trouble. He was impatient, for the tide was running in very fast, and they had to hurry, hurry, to get back to the wreck with their fish. Fine couldn't move at all. William dropped his catch for the moment, caught Fine round the waist, and lifted him to his feet; and there Fine stood, immobilized. William, his arm round Fine's waist, tried to support him and walk him back through the tide, now racing; but Fine started to fall all over the place. His legs wouldn't support him. It was the onset of polyneuritis, a diffuse and symmetrical involvement of nerves, induced by the absence of substances in his diet needed to support the functions of nerves. In the classic tradition, the symptoms had begun with the feet.

Though he did not know it, Fine Feuiaki was sick indeed; but he had no complaint except that he could not move. The tide was coming in so rapidly, and William himself at this time felt so weak that he doubted whether he could get Fine home, but he tried.

He took Fine's fish and added them to his own. Then he lowered Fine into the water, and towed him too. In his other hand he held the harpoon, and they had not gone far before he realized that he would need it, for a large shark, nosing along after the trailed fish, came in his steps.

He threw a crayfish to the shark, but it hardly interrupted the predator's progression, though it opened its mouth to swallow it. He threw another, and another, hoping that soon it would be satisfied and turn away; but it absorbed each thrown crayfish and followed after, shortening its range with increasing confidence. By this time William was up to his hips in water, with no refuge nearer than the wreck, and therefore highly vulnerable; though not as vulnerable as Fine, who occupied all his thoughts. He asked Fine to make a special effort, to try and stand, and drew him up so that he could find his feet; and somehow, for a moment, Fine balanced on his nerveless limbs, then slowly collapsed.

But before he did so, the shark had cruised in within

three feet of where William stood; and William had raised the harpoon, and then delivered it. It was the first shark of William's life; he had never encountered such an emergency in his carpentering; but he hit it true. He speared the shark with both hands, the hammer-flanged point lodging between and above the eyes, and stilling the little brain of the fish, though not its flurries.

When he speared it William pushed down hard, pinning the shark to the broken coral and the sand where they fought; he picked up chunks of coral and hammered its head; and to his amazement, for he was frightened, he won the encounter.

Then he took Fine again and lifted his head above the water. He took the fish and Fine and the shark all together in his left hand, and in his right he took the harpoon, and so he towed this mixed freight back towards the Japanese wreck.

But there his companions had seen his fix; they came out of the boat to the waist-deep, shark-ridden water, and took his burdens from him, and gave him the chance to rest. The shark was eight feet long, the largest of the eighteen sharks the castaways caught upon the reef.

Fine Feuiaki was five weeks in bed from that moment; he could do no more, and augmented the lists of the sick. For the moment these were changing lists, but becoming familiar, since they were the same men who apparently suffered most: Fine, and little Finau Laione, and Fetaiaki Pulu.

Soakai was upset. His basic trouble was probably centred in the indispositions of his son Fetaiaki, for whom he had a great love; but he had a dream also at this time that disturbed him. From the black velvet of his sleep he found himself criticizing his wife, angry at her, indignant that she had had death ceremonies conducted for him. In Tonga pigs are killed at death ceremonies; and in his dream Soakai said, "You fool. We are both alive, Fetaiaki and me; and now as a result of your haste, your foolishness, we have lost our pigs." But his wife told him the fault was none of hers. She hadn't been agreeable to holding the ceremonies, but Soakai's brothers had insisted; they had wanted to do this thing.

In their practical lives the castaways were still getting fish. At one high tide Talo, leaning out of the space that had been a bridge window on the fishing-boat, speared a five-foot tuna. Weeks before Teiapa'a, now almost proficient in the water, had caught with his hands a turtle of which the shell measured two feet across. He had brought it home triumphantly and set it down before the crowd. They could eat it all, he said; but he wanted the shell to take back to Tonga. It was no mean feat to capture a turtle by hand; and the fact that he had chased it up into the shallows of a reef pool didn't detract from the glory of the catch.

David and Ve'etutu had a quarrel now. The low tide was late in the day and the fishing party did not get back to the wreck until after dark; so David decided that they would cook the fish only, leaving the crayfish and the clams until the morning. Ve'etutu, who'd had a hard day, wanted to cook everything that evening; he'd set his heart on a mixed chowder with the addition of the rice flour. When this was denied he got the sulks; he said that he wouldn't eat anything at all in that case, and he wouldn't take his water ration either

David got angry. Ve'etutu was breaking discipline, he said. He told him never again, in his hearing, to say such things as he had said. "If I hear that kind of talk again," David promised, "I'll personally rip you apart; I'll tear your body into two pieces."

Then he went off to his cabin. The incident ended without resentment. Although the boys discussed it intensively, they came to no decision as to the rights of the matter.

About this time the second real rain of their stay came to the party's relief. Again it came at night; it poured in torrents, and from the spread sails they collected nine full spherical floats of water; forty gallons or more, enough to keep them several days on their meagre ration. Talo, at his private catchment, was filling a little trough which had been the casing of some engine part; perhaps of a shaft coupling; its capacity was that of four twenty-six ounce beer bottles. Talo filled it twice and drank it twice, each time without putting it down from his lips, the faster to get it filled again. When he filled it for the third time his father, who with others had seen this feat, took it from him; but Talo never admitted feeling the slightest discomfort from this mighty draught.

Meantime the *Tuaikaepau* raft was getting shipshape; there was a lot of excitement about the possibility of going to sea, and a lot of talk. David ordered a mast raised on the raft; and then he had a canvas painted with the notice about lost men on Minerva Reef. They made a good elaborate job of it, and he had the message duplicated on the planks of the raft.

The workers were beginning to feel, as all this was completed, that the next move would be for David to pick them out—"You and you and you"—the sea-going crew for the raft. Instead he told them to push it out to sea with its messages. It drifted off; they watched it a long time into the distance; and then there was no more talk of leaving the reef.

But immediately David broached his plan of building a small sailing-boat; a boat that would carry a selected crew to Tonga or Fiji to bring help for the others. There was now no chance that an organized search would reach them. They had to arrange for their own deliverance; and the means was at hand if they could build the boat. David himself would captain the expedition, he said; and perhaps they would draw lots for the other two places. He and his two boys, Talo and Sateki, had on 1st August taken an oath publicly that they would die, if that were necessary, to save the lives of the other fourteen; and the voyage would entail some risk.

Soakai here pointed out to them all that all their searches, either on the Japanese ship or at the site of the *Tuaikaepau* wreck, had failed to locate any tools with which they could build. He suggested that some effort might be made to contrive swim-goggles in order to search the depths more thoroughly. The box of tools they had carried on *Tuaikaepau* must still exist; and, since their theory was that it had gone down to the bottom of a certain deep hole, goggles might enable it to be recovered.

David gave due attention to this suggestion, and turned the task of thinking out a substitute for swim goggles over to William Fa. It is said that the worst part of the inventor's trade is thinking out something that needs inventing; certainly William was adequate to the remainder.

Dark and swarthy, his face mottled with the old scars of an adolescent acne, William was a thin, soft-spoken bachelor about thirty-four years of age. He had weighed 174 pounds when they sailed from Tonga, but had been whittled down alarmingly; at this stage he had lost more than forty pounds, as near as they could estimate. He had a capacity for thinking things out; even when it came to stealing water, the method he found successful was by far the least detectable. He simply distorted the count while he was filling the containers. Taking a glass at a time from the delivery end of the still, he was supposed to count aloud so that the others might check the count against him. At some stage he would simply duplicate the last figure he had spoken; preferably after a little small-talk had taken the others' minds from the subject. He would count, for instance, "Six . . . seven . . . eight . . . eight . . . nine", and if this passed without comment from the others he knew that a glassful could later on be extracted from the container without risk of investigation.

William could see possibilities in a supply of two-inch diameter hose which they were using at times for fuel to brighten up the fire. There were also some transparent plastic folders designed to keep working papers clean from wet or fishy hands; they were of fairly heavy quality and would serve as a glass substitute. He first of all cut a round lens and fitted it to a single short length of hose, fitting the hose with a cord harness so that it could be worn by a diver over one eye. He cut the lens from the plastic and fitted it to the open end of the hose, making a socket in the hose, and sealing the joints with pitch melted from the tops of the useless Japanese batteries. But this fabrication was too awkward and inefficient.

His next procedure was to flatten two three-inch sections of hose, holding them to an oval rather than a round shape with twitches of copper wire. To the ends of these flattened sections, wired together in a frame to resemble, somewhat, a pair of field-glasses, he fitted other oval lenses of plastic, sealing them in in the same manner. A harness of cord, as before, fitted the contraption to the diver's eyes. The glasses still leaked at the eyes; and a subject who was a good diver went under water time and time again until all these leaks had been found, and eliminated by cutting the rubber to shape.

William made three sets of such glasses, and the search for tools was redoubled. He made still another pair, a foot or more in length, with the idea that they could be used from a boat or raft, with a man above looking through them to the depths of the water; but this idea was unsuccessful.

A difficulty in finding the tools was that they had been

123

kept in a box all together. The hole in the reef over which the stern of the *Tuaikaepau* had been poised was deep; it was wedge-shaped, too, catching every swirl of water. None of the divers as yet had been able to bottom it; and on most days, when there was a big surf, it was hopeless even to make a serious attempt to get down.

The task of sending out messages was now abandoned. The light wood was needed for the fire for distilling water; though distilling also had been abandoned while rainwater remained, and when it was resumed they distilled only every second day. The fire had to be maintained in some degree, but, with a concentration of effort aimed at building a boat, the task of getting fuel was becoming too great. The planks for the projected boat would have to be cut out of the heavy timber of the Japanese planks; they measured six by two inches in a variety of lengths, and the simple job of removing them from the timbers beneath was frighteningly hard. It took four men working for an hour or more to recover a single plank.

All the men looked to David for strength, and it was David who showed them how things must be done. David himself looked to his God; he had lost his rosary in the wreck, but at three in the morning and four in the afternoon each day he counted off his prayers on his fingers, one "Our Father" and ten "Hail Marys" five times over. On bad days, when it was hot and there was no relief from the sun in their wood and metal prison, and the signs of trouble flickered around the little company like wildfire in the evening hills, he would say more. These prayers were for his solitude; they gave him more personal strength than the prayer meetings he held with such great regularity for his little community.

When there were nights of storm, and their unchancy perch rolled and rocked, disturbing them on their slanted couches, he intensified his prayers. He prayed to St Joseph,

124

his patron saint, and to Saint Teresa, in whose church he had been married; and he took some strength in knowing that his wife Alapasita and his children were also praying. Every night he imagined them at their devotions, saying in Tongan, "Jesus, Mary and Joseph, keep our father and our brother safe." He knew that if he were to lose his strength only a miracle could save the men on the reef; he knew how they looked to him, and he felt the responsibility. He had to display a strength greater than even the best men amongst the others could show.

In a distilling group consisting of Vaiangina, Teiapa'a, and Saia Peni, and led by Ve'etutu, an argument developed between Saia and Teiapa'a. They came to blows. There was a short scuffle and the mate intervened. But Vaiangina said, "No. Let them fight. Let them settle this thing once and for all and it will stop their bickering."

So the two of them fought. There was some bad blood thickening between them and the blows came too hard and too viciously. The mate leapt up to stop them; and while he was in the thick of the struggle Vaiangina grabbed the container of water and started drinking for dear life. After the fight was stopped the mate stared at the lowered level of the bottle and asked where the water had gone. Vaiangina said he'd managed to save that amount; the rest had got tipped over in the scuffle—for he had taken the precaution of dampening the floor to support his statements. There was nothing that the men would not do to ease their sufferings; but the captain stole no water and broke no rules.

He was thinking, at this time, of the crew he would select for the voyage when the boat was made; a boat that as yet was only a series of developing plans. His first impulse was to take Soakai, for one. He told Soakai about it and they talked it over, but on the following day David said it would be better, he thought, if Soakai were to help to control the men who would be left on the reef, and asked him to think about it.

Soakai saw Ve'etutu, and asked him how he thought he'd get on with the boys if trouble should develop after the captain had gone. Ve'etutu replied that if any were silly enough to make trouble to the pitch where they'd attack him, he'd simply hit them on the head with the nearest length of timber. Soakai decided that it would be better for him to stay on the reef; he thought that he could be a peacemaker.

But as peacemaker Ve'etutu was perhaps better than Soakai. Ve'etutu was quick and active, and ranged the reef on every opportunity; he never had a day's illness, and the only resentment he caused was that sometimes he would stand over the distilling gang and insist on getting a mouthful of water. He didn't ask, he ordered; and some of the lads felt that he did not show a proper responsibility in giving way to this weakness.

A day or so after the boat decision was made Soakai was sick. He knows he wasn't really sick; he reported sick because of the dispiriting effects of his annoyance with the boys (and in fact his annoyance with them was that they were human, and acted like humans, displaying human weaknesses). Lying down, feigning sickness, Soakai got remorseful; his conscience was troubling him. He kept thinking of the oath the Fifitas had made; he knew that his own contribution to the common cause was less than it might have been, and he determined to do something to retrieve himself in his own eyes.

He determined to find the box of tools, though it meant diving deeper and more dangerously than anyone else could. And certainly he tried, and kept trying. But in this too he failed. At other times, when they were confined to the wreck, he worked like a madman, trying to strip the planks from their fastenings.

The day they started building the boat the men were told to get sufficient timber for the seven V-frames that would sit upon the keelson. By the end of the day they had only two. David called them together after a prayer meeting, and told them that the progress was too slow. Soakai recommended that David set them a definite amount for each day, and institute whippings for whoever did less than his share, together with a reduction of rations. David told them if they didn't work the next day there would certainly be a tougher regimen introduced. Next day they got the seven frames together.

There was now a constant work upon the wreck whenever daylight held and the condition of the ocean, which at high tide and in stormy weather rocked the wreck, permitted. This work was interrupted by the low tide, when it was necessary to fish and to search for anything useful. Their powers were also limited by the necessity of looking after the sick.

But grey-eyed Minerva, the patroness of handicrafts, of the arts and the trades and invention, had no more significant temples on the Capitoline or the Aventine than on this her reef; invention and ingenuity were called upon for the provision of every small necessity of every day.

Under their handicap of complete isolation, under the need to produce a sea-going vessel with little more than their fingers for tools, these men, most of them, responded admirably. Nor did they neglect the care of their weaker fellows.

Poor Fatai seemed to rally somewhat when the building of the boat began. He was wasting away to the point where his physical condition was nothing less than shocking, but for a while now he became more rational, and no longer needed a guard to watch his movements. He was a communicant of the Church of Tonga, but earlier in his life he had been, for a time, a Roman Catholic, and he began to attend the Catholic prayer meetings in David's cabin; almost the only cabin left in the ship now, and rapidly itself becoming part of the larger compartment, as linings and floorings went to the upkeep of the fire.

Fine Feuiaki was still bedridden, though he seemed to be slowly regaining the use of his limbs. Also on the seriously sick list were Johnny Sikimeti and Soakai's son Fetaiaki. Some of the others thought that Soakai was adopting the wrong tactics with his son; they thought he should get him out more often, and that Fetaiaki could have contributed more to the common weal.

Finau Laione was just as sick as some of the others, they thought, but he was irrepressible, running around as lively as though he were a kid on holiday. He tried to make himself a part of every enterprise, he attempted to do things that were far beyond his failing strength. To look at he was just skin and bone.

William Fa was by no means well. But he was essential to the boat-building enterprise. David Uaisele was in charge of the actual carpentering operations, but to William fell the task of measuring out and marking planks for later shaping, and of devising methods for doing the work.

He collapsed frequently when the sun was hot; and he says he will never forget the captain's kindness; David Fifita was ever thoughtful of him and, when he felt faint or had been doing too much, would carry him to a resting-place in the shade. David himself had lost a great deal of weight and no longer felt strong. He had been the biggest of them all, but his privations, some of them self-imposed, were greater than anyone else's.

Teiapa'a Bloomfield, on the other hand, was becoming one of the group's more useful members. He was on the reef a lot with Vaiangina and Ve'etutu; he had lost hardly any weight, and was managing to get enjoyment from his swimming and fishing, occupations to which he had been entirely a stranger.

The sustenance of the sick was beginning to weigh heavily upon the well. There was an occasion when Fatai Efiafi began to fail again, and Talo was at the fire frying a fish in the oil from its liver. David told him to give the fish to Fatai. Talo said he would do so, and David went on elsewhere. When he returned Fatai had still not been fed; and Talo had eaten the fish and was in process of cooking another. David was tired of admonitions; he hit Talo on the head with a billet of firewood, slapped his face hard and walked away. It was the nearest approach to anger he had shown. It was also the first physical punishment he had inflicted.

William Fa had a dream. He dreamt he was in Tonga, standing in the garden of the Royal Palace, down by the waterfront; and he could see Queen Salote talking from the tower. He could see her clearly, but couldn't hear what she was saying. He thought about that dream a long time, trying to find significance in it, but in the end he decided it didn't have any.

Another time, about this same period, he was standing outside a Tongan house where a number of people were singing. He listened to the song a long time; it was a strange one that he couldn't recognize, and the only words he could distinguish were: "And all the people on earth shall enter."

Vaiangina dreamt that he saw a sailing-boat approaching the South Minerva Reef. He said to others standing round: "This is our salvation; they have come to take us back." The others in the cabin heard him. But only his shout had reality. The dream was so vivid he was distressed when he woke up and found that it was not true.

But Teiapa'a dreamt he was in Tonga, walking along the level road, lively with people who were just not near enough to him. He saw his brother coming, not in the taxi that he normally drove, but in a cart piled high with coconuts, green coconuts, for drinking. His brother threw him a coconut, which he drank. It was a big coconut, so big he couldn't finish it. And when he woke from that dream his thirst was slaked; he didn't feel thirsty for some hours afterwards.

Then David Fifita had a dream. He found himself back in Ha'apai talking to his wife, and the day was Friday. He had just come into the house from somewhere, just returned from a voyage, perhaps, and he saw a beautiful mango, a large mouth-watering mango ripe and ready for eating. He said to Alapasita, "You'd better eat it." But she said, "No. I'll keep it till Tuesday, for on Tuesday a man is bringing me a can of meat."

He felt, when he woke up, that this was an omen. When in the morning he saw the whole crew at his prayer meeting he told them of his dream after the service. At that Talo spoke up; that night, he said, he also had had a dream, and he also had dreamed of Alapasita. But in his dream the message was more direct. All she said was, "Be sure you come home Tuesday."

"Mark it," Fifita said. "You wait and see. Whatever will happen to us will happen on a Tuesday."

A lot was to happen to them, but it was a Tuesday that turned out to be the best day of their lives.

Chapter Nine

IN Tonga, about the second week in September, three boys
—two of them fourteen years old, the other young at
seventeen—disappeared, and with them disappeared the
fishing-boat *Vaisingano*. She was an open whaler, 32 feet
in length with a beam of eight, and well furnished with
four sweeps, a mast and sails, two anchors and fifteen
fathoms of chain. She also carried a compass.

There was a good deal of anxiety in Tonga, until such
time as a message to the Tonga Government came over
the air from the mother-ship of a Japanese fishing-fleet.
The message was dated 17th September 1962 and read:

"Our fishing-boat *Monju Maru* Number Five rescued
three Tonga boys at 1550 S 17740 W on 2230 hours six-
teenth. Stop. Their name and age Pangia seventeen, Tan-
ginoa fourteen, Paso fourteen and they lived in Nuku'alofa
stop."

The message was signed "Nojimamaru".

The boys were pupils of the Mormon College at Laihona,

a few miles out of Nuku'alofa. It is perhaps one of the attractions of the Mormon creed in the islands that it offers to able and selected pupils the chance of travel; and in these days the radio, the air services, the increasing numbers of visitors are making young Tongans conscious of the physical limitations and the close-set boundaries of their kingdom. Some Mormon students finish their training in Hawaii, where there is now a growing colony of Tongans, and still others get to the United States, a not quite believable land of El Dorado, if Tongans can judge by the spending-habits of the American citizens they see.

So these lads had stolen the boat with the intention of reaching the United States. They had stocked it with some food, and had travelled quite a way, past the Ha'apai group where Captain Cook landed, past Tofua and Kao, where Bligh was set adrift by the *Bounty* mutineers, past Vava'u and out of the Tonga group proper, and about eighty-five miles further on to the proximity of Niuafo'ou, that Tin Can Island of which Tofa Ramsay's father wrote in his book.

It was a wild night when they were picked up. The Japanese skipper took the *Vaisingano* in tow, but the weather was against this enterprise, and halfway through the night she had to be cut adrift. Tongans rejoiced for the safety of the lads; but the loss of the *Vaisingano* made them sad; she was a staunch ship and had been built by David Uaisele, who at this moment was in process of building his most famous vessel on the South Minerva Reef.

No one in Tonga was to know that. Outside the close relatives of some of the men, everyone had given up hope. Their abundant faith in David Fifita's abilities had faded with the passing weeks, and there were some already who were urging relatives to apply for a legal decision that the seventeen missing men were dead.

Outside the Tongan group interest had altogether waned,

though the September issue of the *Pacific Islands Monthly*, a periodical with a wide-spread range of influence covering the entire South Pacific, reported:

Tuaikaepau, a 45-foot yacht owned by Tofa Ramsay of Nuku'alofa, was reported overdue on a voyage from Tonga to Auckland on July 30, and was still missing in mid-August. The yacht left Tonga on July 4 and was believed to have seventeen people on board. She was carrying a ton of groceries, 144 gallons of water and other stores. The yacht's master, Tevita Fifita, is believed to have intended fishing near 'Ata, the southernmost island of the Tonga group, which is uninhabited. After aircraft from New Zealand unsuccessfully searched for the yacht early in August, the Air-Sea Rescue Organisation called off the search until more definite information on the vessel's movements was received.

In the October issue a similar notice was followed by a supplementary paragraph:

After an unsuccessful air search for the yacht early in August, Tonga Radio reported that an unknown craft carrying a large number of people had been sighted about August 10 near the island of Niuatoputapu, about 150 miles north-east of Vava'u and about 500 miles from 'Ata. All boats in the area were asked to look out for the yacht.

Though they knew nothing of these moves, the *Tuaikaepau* men were convinced that their only hope now lay in the vessel they were building. She had been planned at an approximate eighteen feet of length and four feet six inches of beam, with a chine bottom centred by a keel with eighteen inches of depth; for in all probability she would have to sail close to the wind.

A shipyard was the castaways' immediate problem. She could not be built on the reef, and the Japanese wreck itself, crowded as to its usable parts, had to provide a working area. The largest space was outside, on the beam; but exposure to wind and weather made the use of this impracticable. Instead they cleared a space on the port quarter, and on the metal side of the house they laid down the blocks on which she was to be built. A fierce heat was reflected from the metal; there was no refuge from the sun; but it was the only site available.

All the skilled work had to be done by David Uaisele or William Fa; there was little that the others could contribute. Sometimes, indeed, two men were too many, for their tools consisted of a knife with a serrated edge, the chisel-ended spike, and the hammer. Since the materials they were to use were the heavy pine planks of the wreck, each cut was an ordeal.

William shortened the process by remembering the ways of his ancestors in using fire. They heated an iron bar that had a straight edge a quarter-inch wide, and held this along the cut to be made until, after several applications, it had bitten in to a depth of half an inch or so. The char was cleaned out with the spike, and when burning was no longer effective the spike became a chisel, and was driven down another inch, working gradually the length of the cut, the operator moving it as he drove to keep it loose in the socket it created. When this process was complete the board was held over an edge of decking parallel to the half-formed cut, and a heavy blow with the rifle-butt broke it off. The knife and the hammer smoothed off the edges.

By whatever miracle of patience and persistence they managed to cut the rabbets running the length of the stem-post only they themselves know; the grooves were extended to their final shape until the stem took on the appearance of a professional job; its forward edge chamfered to cut the waves, the rabbets at its bottom extension aligned exactly with the corresponding grooves in the keel, and all this done with the six-inch spike. The seven V-frame floors were fitted to the keel and keelson; and soon there was the skeleton of a little ship, deadwoods all true, fastenings driven and clenched.

Fifita meanwhile was looking for a mast. He discovered a stout twenty-foot bamboo—where is the Japanese vessel in the world without its emergency supplies of cane and bamboo?—and served the ends with tarred cord against the chance of its splitting.

He and Soakai, and indeed every able-bodied man not needed elsewhere, went as frequently as the weather allowed to try to recover the tools from the wreck. On one occasion Soakai saw a crayfish in a pool and dived in, to haul it out by its feelers and hand it up to David. He saw another while he was there, and pulled that out. Standing in the one place, pulling out crayfish after crayfish, he handed them up to David until the captain said, "That's enough". He had seventeen, one for every man of their party, so plentiful were they.

The building of the boat monopolized the fire and the available firewood. When it came to steaming the planks they could not contrive a steam-box, nor did they have any G-clamps to hold the planks in position, and finish the shaping of them by pressure.

Instead they collected all the rags, all the rotten tarpaulin, every kind of cloth available for their purpose. They soaked each plank in the sea all night, tethering it to the ship; and when it was well soaked they carried it up on deck. Even that was difficult; the planks were heavy, and the precipitous slope of the stripped deck made it a hazard even to move. Young Finau Laione, trying to be of service as his habit was, slipped from the upper part of the deck where the boat-building was going on, and thought himself dead, for there was a twenty-foot fall beneath. But his fingers caught the edge of the decking, and a lot of friendly hands were swift to pull him up again.

The rags were soaked in boiling sea-water and wrapped tight around the plank to be bent at the places where the bend was to be effective. They worked at speed, to lose as little as possible of the heat. An end of the plank was tommed and wedged between the rail of the ship and the house; they used two or three toms if the length of straight planned for the plank allowed.

Rope lashed to the other end was made fast and twitched, so that a great strain pulled the plank into its curve from the straightness it had held since the tree was cut, long years before. They had to watch the strain; the planks were precious for the energy it took to recover them; and when a plank had taken all it could, fresh applications of the heated, steaming rags were necessary. Some of the planks had to be bent two ways at once, and wedges were driven in at various points to accomplish this; the finished plank was as shapely as any from a professional yard, though the accomplishment cost infinitely more in effort.

Since the planks were of pine, the carpenters had little trouble driving the nails and clenching them; the chamfering necessary to prepare for the driving of asbestos caulking (which David had discovered in the paint store on his first day in the wreck) was a painful task with hammer and table-knife.

The spike served as caulking-iron too; both the spike and the knife applied the putty.

Between the fire and the sun's heat they worked at a point close to exhaustion; and three times William Fa lost consciousness. There were no dissentients when David Fifita allotted both craftsmen a tiny issue of extra water; all their lives lay in the carpentry, and every man aboard knew it. In an amazingly short time, a matter of between two and three weeks, the hull took shape, but much remained to do.

For sails Fifita intended to use the jib and the staysail

136

from *Tuaikaepau*. They had recovered them with the mast on that first night when they were wrecked, and had used them in the rains to catch the water. The sails required adjustment, and David did what he could in this matter.

When anything in the boat-building task required strength Vaiangina and Sipa Fine were at hand; these two and Uaisele, Ve'etutu and Teiapa'a were now among the fittest men left; but Ve'etutu and Teiapa'a had their hands full with fishing. Boat construction had meant that the castaways could not pay full attention to the larder. Those who were not occupied with the actual building still had their water-distilling to take care of, and the sick.

Sometimes there was a spare moment, and the captain urged the men to devote such time to prayer. Teiapa'a got hold of one of the many small exercise books lying around, and sometimes wrote in it a letter home; a letter that he knew would never be delivered. But when the captain sailed, he thought, he would send a letter. Some of his writings have been preserved in the book where he set them down, on pages already covered with small, neat Japanese characters. They are addressed to members of his family, people and places he loved:

> *Sunia. Eta. Halamahi. Mele. Etimoa.*
> *I love you all. I am all right here.*
> > *Teiapa'a Bloomfield.*

And:

> *Maeaki. Sela. Sione. Valenisia. Motolilo. Saane. Tonga. Alaveini.*
> *How are you now? I hope you are all right there.*
> > *Teiapa'a Bloomfield.*

Sunia was his father, Maeaki his brother, Sela his sister-in-law, Tonga his country.

They are brave letters. They make no complaints except perhaps for the implied one of an overwhelming homesickness. And they are testimonials of faith, for among the survivors from South Minerva Reef there was not a single man who had any doubt of his return. William Fa, who thinks a lot about their experiences—and who among them can refrain?—believes that their great faith was developed and encouraged by the fact that everyone talked of survival, everyone thought of survival all the time. They would talk for hours about what they would eat when they got back, whom they would visit, and how their future lives would be conducted.

The little ship grew fast, though every feature of it seemed to introduce a fresh problem. The rudder gudgeons, for instance, were a worry. They had to take a great strain. They were fashioned of nails bent over into staple form, and those attached to the hull were driven right through the wood and clenched on the other side; but those on the rudder itself could not be clenched, and the men had to trust to luck that they would hold.

The chain-plates for the rigging were made in a similar way. Every part of the boat was as staunch as though she were meant to live a hundred years; nothing was scamped, nothing let do for the emergency. The best of their materials, the best of their labour went into her.

When the hull was complete they decked her over, leaving a hatch five feet long and two feet wide abaft the mast. A man, or two men, could crawl in there and sleep, away from the weather. They spent days cutting the short planks that decked her in, making them tight, finishing off.

Along the seams they nailed copper strip over the putty-coated caulking. They raised the mast, and made provision for the flag of Tonga, a red Geneva cross in a white canton on a red field. They were very proud of it, and with reason, as they were proud of their boat. As a last step they painted its name on the bow—*Malolelei*, and on the stern the name, "St Joseph". "My body-saint," said David Fifita.

Malolelei had been the name of David's father's ship, which in its time became David's first command. "Malolelei" is the common greeting of Tonga, a gracious greeting, "Thank you for being well", and usually translated "Good Morning". It was a pert name for a staunch vessel. In later days newspapers were to describe *Malolelei* as a raft, but there was nothing raft-like about her. She was the product of proud boat-builders who could not do less than their best on the excuse of having no tools.

Malolelei was complete, but there remained the heaviest task of all: launching her from her eyrie at the top of the Japanese vessel. She weighed a ton; later when she arrived in Tonga from Fiji twenty-five men lifted her, and carried her with some effort along the level wharf; but here on Minerva Reef she had to be launched, without damage, down the precipitous cliff of deck-beam edges to the water. They were ten men, ten men who were fit; and their lives depended on the safety of the boat.

The twin masts of the wreck stuck out almost horizontally, pointing towards the northern coast of the reef. From the triatic stay which connected the masts near their trucks, a stout steel cable still in excellent condition, David had a series of single pulleys suspended. To balance this pull and centralize the lift they shored up the awning stanchions on the port rail abeam of the well-deck, ahead of where *Malolelei* sat on her blocks. A lift was arranged with pulleys at each of these two stanchions. To control the pull, when the weight of the little ship should be launched into space between the triatic stay and the stanchions, they affixed other blocks to a heavy cleat aft.

David stationed Vaiangina here, with the rope controlling *Malolelei's* movement. Sipa Fine was in charge of the rope that constituted the fall through the series of blocks on the triatic stay. Ve'etutu watched the haul on the after stanchion, and Talo that from the forward one. David was in charge of the operation, and all other able-bodied men disposed themselves according to his orders as the changing situation warranted.

Inch by inch they shifted the ship from the cradle of her birth. When she was halfway they took new purchases, and got her down to the water. She floated beautifully; and there began immediately the new task of ballasting her with any iron they could lay their hands on. They had a girder running more than half her length, and other pieces contributing to a total of about half a ton of ballast.

The concerted effort was almost too much for William Fa, now one of the worst of the sick. When *Malolelei* had been launched and he was no longer essential he took to his bed; he was exhausted. He was completely willing to leave the rest to David. All along he had felt that the leadership they had been given on the reef was of the best; he had a feeling for the captain that was composed of admiration and affection, and he had sufficient appreciation of the difficulties to know that the captain had had the hardest task of any of them.

For his part, and David Uaisele's, William was satisfied. They had put everything possible into the boat; they had made as good a job as it was possible to make, and it had taken all his strength. He felt that the effort, and the experience which had called it forth, had had a lasting effect on his personal life; that hereafter religion would play a much greater part in it. He resolved to take more interest in the affairs of his Wesleyan Church, and try to achieve some prominence among its supporters.

Soakai and Sipa Fine and Ve'etutu made one more trip to the site of the *Tuaikaepau* wreck. Sipa Fine and Ve'etutu were wearing the glasses that William Fa had contrived, and when they came to the site they dived and dived.

Soakai had the third set; by this time one of the lenses had come loose and they were no longer of much use; it was a discipline to use them in any way in which he could see effectively.

But he was still obsessed with his desire to do something that would be of vital help; something that matched in nobility the sentiments the captain had expressed when, nearly two months before, he and his two sons had sworn to die, if necessary, to save the lives of the others. He was determined to penetrate the hole where, they thought, the tools had slipped down.

The other two dived first, and as ineffectively as on all the previous attempts. Then Soakai tried. To get where he thought he would find results he had to dive through the break of a wave. He went well down, successfully negotiating the hazards near the surface, and at three fathoms, in the swirl occasioned by the wedge-shaped cavity in the reef, he saw the *Tuaikaepau's* engine lying on top of a big drum. Drums were valuable, each one could carry another message out into the ocean; but he could see that this one was so badly holed as to be useless.

He came up again, pulled himself on top of the reef, and dived down through the surge. He positioned himself at the engine and, clinging to it, felt all around amongst the coral. His fingers closed on the handle of a cane-knife, previously unseen, and he brought it to the top.

It would have been a sovereign implement in the building of the boat, and as it was the carpenters could use it to smooth some of the roughness that their lack of tools had forced them to leave; for the knife was in good condition, and they could put an edge on it.

Fatai had been very weak on these days, and David was not sure that he was getting the best of attention, so he ordered him brought to his cabin. Fatai just lay there and seemed to be getting weaker; but he also seemed to enjoy the benefit of the Catholic services which David conducted night and morning, and sometimes oftener. Whenever there was anything to fear, whenever there was anything to celebrate, whenever there was an occasion for thanksgiving, David took the matter to his God; and in their mood upon this waste of waters his actions had the approbation of all his fellows.

On 28th September, at the evening prayer meeting, Fatai seemed to listen with a real intensity. He was too weak and ill to sit up; he was lying on his side facing David; and he continued to lie like that throughout the prayers. When they were finished he stayed still; the prayer had been a thanksgiving for the evening meal, and David told Talo to take Fatai some fish. When Talo approached him, Fatai took no notice. After his period of coherence he had relapsed again into a pattern of inconsequential actions, and this looked like just another variation on the pattern. But when Talo shook him, Fatai fell back. He was dead.

In the Tongan fashion they set a fire, and kept vigil with the body throughout the night. In the morning they dug a grave three hundred yards away from the wreck, in a place where coral boulders rested upon sand and broken shingle. They dug it with their hands and with iron bars, and they could not dig it deep; but for anyone who knows the composition and texture of a coral reef the marvel is that they could dig a grave at all.

They had a fear that the crabs and fish on which they would later subsist would eat the body; they had a horror that they might be guilty of cannibalism at a remove; and they used some tarpaulin to wrap the poor, wasted body. They wrapped it three times round and bound it tightly with fathoms of the tarred fishing-line that still remained within the wreck. And after they had lowered Fatai into the grave and covered him up, and David had conducted a burial service, they marked his resting-place with a cross.

The death of Fatai made them feel the urgency of their task; but David was not yet ready to sail. He wanted to get some stores of fish and water together for his journey; more than that, he wanted to test out the capacity of his craft, and when he had done so he was not satisfied. She was a little unstable. The absence of a toe-rail made it difficult to cling to her deck in any violence of motion; and he knew that at any target island available to him there was an encircling reef. He was afraid of what might happen if that deep keel should touch. Finally he decided that he would redesign the boat, remove the keel, and substitute an outrigger.

This decision made him vulnerable, he knew, to the vagaries of the weather. An outrigger must ride to windward; in the ancient sailing vessels of the Pacific the hull which did not carry the sail was always to windward; the process of tacking meant switching bow for stern, and as a result both ends of the boat had to be fitted with a steering mechanism.

To run to Fiji, to the nearest island of Ono-i-Lau, David would have to set his outrigger to starboard and depend upon a south-east wind. If the wind should switch, since he could not substitute bow for stern, he would be at its mercy, and might be carried over countless miles of ocean, willy-nilly.

Moreover, the season in which he could depend on a south-east wind was coming to an end. The Trades are not constant in the Central Pacific, and the variable winds may be reckoned to begin in October. He was making a gamble of it, but since life is a gamble, since he had little choice, and since, to be successful, he had in some way to steady the boat, he decided upon this rebuilding.

Malolelei could not be lifted again to her yard at the top of the Japanese wreck; therefore they had to make a yard of sorts on the beach at the wreck's base. They set about finding a drum that would take the stern of the little ship, filling it with sand and setting it on a platform; they arranged a niche for her nose on the deck of the Jap, and brought her there at high tide to lift her above the reach of the sea.

David set Vaiangina and Talo to cleaning out the ballast which, with an outrigger, was no longer necessary, and which would interfere with lifting *Malolelei* to her new perch. Talo got into the hatchway of the little vessel and began handing out the ballast, piece by piece, to Vaiangina.

"Vaiangina deceived me; he told me a lie," David remembered later. "He told me he had cleaned the boat out, but there was still about three hundredweight of iron left in the stern of her. I thought that a couple of nights in the water had given her the extra weight." But they got her up, lifting her a little above the top of the tide, themselves waist- and shoulder-deep in water.

They cut off nearly all the keel, leaving a short projection only about three inches deep, and not running the full length of the boat. With the cane-knife that Soakai had recovered from the pool they chopped down the foremast of the Japanese wreck, and from its upper part they hacked out a section just a foot or so shorter than *Malolelei*, and got ready three transverse beams to fasten it to the hull. The beams were six-by-two planks, just like the planks they had built into the little ship. They shaped the outrigger, using their eyes as precision instruments; and, when all was ready to commence building, they started to lift *Malolelei* down off the blocks.

That was when Johnny Lousi died. They didn't know, and don't know why he died. One moment he was lifting; the next he had fallen over backwards and was dead. Maybe he hit his head in the fall; but there was nothing to show that the blow was fatal, and so they thought that perhaps his heart had burst with the great effort he was making; they thought he had worked too hard. But they didn't know.

They put *Malolelei* back on her blocks and went up into the wreck to tell the others that Johnny Lousi had died; and Johnny Sikimeti looked at them when they told him, and he died too. One moment they were all there, all but poor dead Fatai, to whose loss they had been resigned for months; the next moment they had lost two more.

The two Johnnys were not the ones they had expected to lose, for they had sensed the close approach of Death. Finau Laione was more sick, more emaciated, more likely to die than Sikimeti, they thought; and Johnny Lousi had seemed in good health.

"It wasn't possible to tell how exposure and underfeeding were affecting the men," David Fifita said weeks later. "For Fatai Efiafi was not sick, but died after slowly wasting away, and he was forty-six years of age. On the other hand, Johnny Sikimeti was only eighteen, but died in exactly the same way. In the case of Johnny Lousi, he died while working, possibly through overexertion. He was only thirty years of age. So it wasn't possible to tell whether the older men or the younger showed the effects most. In my opinion it was not a matter of age, but it was a matter of will-power; that is, the will to survive."

They kept the bodies by them, and watched them beside a night-burning fire. But in the morning they would not bury them. They had not sufficient canvas to ensure that the creatures of the reef would not feed on the bodies, nor did they know how much longer they would have to stay there. And they did not think they could stand up to the gruelling work of digging holes in the coral. So they bound the bodies up, and set floats to keep them on the surface of the sea, and set them adrift.

The little body of Johnny Sikimeti was wrapped in

canvas and buoyed with a Japanese fishing-float. On the canvas they painted a distress message—SOS MEN ON MINERVA REEF—and on the fishing-float itself there was a painted label "Bill"; a misleading label, and only there because the float had belonged, by right of discovery, to William Fa.

For Johnny Lousi they had no canvas and no bottle. They wrapped him in a half-blanket that had come from the Japanese wreck, and they buoyed him with composition floats that the Japanese fishermen had used to set their flags upon the sea's surface.

It fell to Talo Fifita to take the bodies in tow and launch them on their journey. There was a fair tide flowing as he went, and he waded in water high up on his chest, towing Johnny Sikimeti in one hand and Johnny Lousi in the other. He waded a long way, towing them to a pass on the inner side of the reef where the water always flowed to the westward, and there he let them go, bobbing gently and serenely over the calm lagoon, their arms by their sides, their legs straight as on a bier, sailing into the setting sun, in the direction which, from time immemorial, men have believed to be the one taken by the spirits in their journey to another world.

Talo will never lightly forget that task. He had never had anything to do with the dead before, and he is an impressionable lad. He made no complaint at being asked to do it, but it has stayed much in his mind ever since. It has troubled his sleep, and brought a shudder to some reflective moments.

Talo's father David felt the tragedy of the deaths. It added a little to his personal tragedy which at that time was that he had lost a life; for in all his career he had safely guarded all who had been in his care.

But some of the others accepted death with a philosophy

146

undisturbed by the fact that the dead men had been their friends.

Teiapa'a Bloomfield, for example, said later, "I was almost pleased. It lightened the task of looking after the sick; and of course it left more water for the living."

And little Finau Laione, in whom the germs of tuberculosis were at that time flourishing, who stood less chance than any other of coming alive from the reef, was honest in his reactions too. He said, "I really had no more concern than if they had been animals who died. My concern was for myself; I was afraid that I might die before a rescue came. I was always worried about the fact that I was getting weaker, and I never did give myself more than a fifty-fifty chance of survival. So the dead men didn't worry me. And when we kept the night watch by their bodies I went to sleep."

In his sleep he dreamt of home; and the silent men with the bodies heard his voice, chatting happily to the eight younger children of his family, three hundred miles from South Minerva and the reaching fingers of the Dark Angel.

Chapter Ten

THE night of Friday, 5th October, was a fine one in Nuku'alofa, and Tongan sportsmen crowded the open-air arena at the back of Semesi Koloamatangi's store in the main street to see a much-discussed heavyweight fight between Finau Lahi and Fungalea Fifita. The picture theatre was the normal venue for such contests, but the arena was preferred whenever the weather was suitable. Fungalea Fifita was no relation of Captain David's; but Finau Lahi, a 28-year-old who had attracted a good deal of attention, was the illegitimate son of Soakai Pulu, and much beloved by his father, who was proud of his prowess.

The fight went to the fifth round, in which a terrific punch to the jaw lifted Finau off his feet; lifted him so high, in fact, that he sailed through the air in a parabola and the back of his skull hit the canvas first when he landed. He might otherwise have survived the punch, for he had a reputation for taking punishment; but he never recovered consciousness. He was taken to hospital in a taxi, and there he died.

The incident rejuvenated the storm of discussion about Soakai and the other voyagers on *Tuaikaepau*, but the general consensus of opinion now was that those men were for ever lost; the affair had become a mystery of the sea, and it was thought that it would never be solved.

On Minerva Reef, on the same day, the *Malolelei* was ready for her voyage. Fatai Efiafi had died on 28th September, the other two on 30th September. In the meantime the survivors had fitted the *Malolelei* with her outrigger. It was a remarkable piece of engineering.

It is mandatory that an outrigger should "work"; that it should have some capacity for movement independently of the craft to which it is fitted; but the restriction on this independent movement must be strong. The castaways solved the major problem by bending a metal strip and fastening it to the outrigger beam at the ends, and, a foot and a half above this outrigger, to the middle one of the three projecting transverse beams from *Malolelei* at the centre; so that the metal acted as a diagonal stay in either direction, with a certain spring.

This stay ran longitudinally with the outrigger itself; two other strips nailed round the diameter of the outrigger were made fast in two places each to the forward and after transverse beams. Wire lashings which kept these in place ran through sections of heavy rubber hose, to allow of a certain working, to preserve the wire from breaking, and to prevent it loosening by cutting into the timber during the course of the voyage. Another fore-and-aft beam above the outrigger and parallel to it made the construction so tight that no joint had moved when *Malolelei*, after a series of adventures, came to port.

The forward and after stays of the three by which the outrigger was affixed were fastened to both port and starboard sides of the ship with wire lashings in lieu of bolts; the third or centre one would have crossed the hatchway and interfered with its use, and so was fastened only in two places on the starboard side.

Once again, when all was finished, the little ship had to be tried out, and the captain took her into the lagoon. It had been in his mind to explore the reef; a project on which Ve'etutu was very keen; for in his wanderings the mate had seen, just beyond the limits to which his sure legs could carry him, a number of unidentified objects; either coral blocks of very large size and regular shape, or perhaps the remains of wrecks.

But the deaths of the men had lent urgency to the expedition, and there was not much time. The weather now was a little unsettled; it was essential that the *Malolelei* wait for a south-easterly, for this was the only wind that could take her to safety. The party spent a few days waiting for the wind to be committed to this direction; and when David felt that it was ready to blow for a week or so, uninterruptedly, he set out.

He had revised his opinion about selecting a crew by lot. For one thing he would have to have fit men; if he excluded any from the lottery it would cause resentment; for there were some who felt they were more fit than they actually were. Also it was essential, he thought, to leave Ve'etutu in charge of those who stayed; he was fit, and could feed them; he had authority, and he was in any case second-in-command.

David was unsure of his rudder gudgeons; he took the carpenter who was an original crew member and was fit and well: David Uaisele. And for the third man he chose his son Sateki, because Sateki was the best swimmer of them all, as indeed he had demonstrated at the island of 'Ata. It did not matter if two of them died on the *Malolelei*, David argued, so long as the third could get ashore.

He was also uncomfortably aware that, of the islands he could aim for, all had encircling reefs on which *Malolelei* could very well come to grief; and it was necessary that someone should be able to swim the long distance to the shore. Sateki was the choice.

He probably had a more personal reason for selecting these two as companions; for they both were Catholics, and in the utter lack of privacy on the *Malolelei* they could be together in the exercises of their particular creed. Indeed, this may have been the prime reason for the selection; though it is doubtful that any other choice of personnel could have been better.

Malolelei performed satisfactorily on her trials. David made them short, and brought her back to an anchorage within the lagoon, close to the Japanese wreck. From that time, the 1st or 2nd of October, he slept aboard the craft lest some sudden storm should arise.

While the construction of *Malolelei* was coming to an end David worked on his chart. He took a broad plank of dressed pine that he had set aside weeks before, and began to work out a triangulation which would give him a course to Ono-i-Lau. He could remember the course and distance from the eastern tip of Tonga to Ono-i-Lau, the course and distance from the same point to 'Ata, and the course and distance from 'Ata to Minerva. Using the angles on his sextant (which, with the compass and his Nautical Almanac, he had recovered from the *Tuaikaepau*) he drew a diagram which would give him the course and distance from Tonga to Minerva, and, this completing two sides of his essential triangle, the course and distance from Minerva to Ono-i-Lau. This triangulation was unmarked on his wooden chart;

he kept the figures in his head, for he did not want his expedition marred by any of the men taking matters into their own hands and running away with *Malolelei*, or stealing or copying the chart to use on some raft voyage of their own, or even keeping a copy until after he had gone and following him in some vessel of their own contriving.

When he was sure of his calculations he graved them into the board, cutting over the pencil lines. Then, on a larger scale, he transferred the course-line to another part of the board, and graved in these angles. The chart looked like a geometrical diagram; no one else could read it; but on it David could follow his position and set course not only for Ono-i-Lau but for the other islands to which he might have to turn, particularly Matuku, farther north and west, and as a last resort the Fijian island of Kandavu.

There had been a moderate rain during the building of *Malolelei*, and now, on the night of 3rd October, they had their last rain. They saved a supply of water, and from it David took a single float, half full, holding perhaps a couple of gallons, for the voyage. In the afternoon of 4th October the wanted weather settled in; cold weather, with a steady breeze, rather too much easterly in it for David's needs, but a holding breeze that would continue several days. The seas were high, much higher than would be comfortable; but it was not comfort that the men sought.

So sure were they in their faith that the captain would come to land that now the men remaining on the reef all wrote letters to be delivered to their people. Teiapa'a wrote five, to his mother and father and his brothers and sisters. Some of them had written letters before, to sublimate their lonelinesses. William Fa, who was perhaps as lonely as anyone, had not done so, but now he wrote a letter to his brother, just a gesture. What he had to say was, "Send me a bottle of water; send me a water-melon." Saia Peni, the only one of them all to write nothing, sent a verbal message to his brother: "Send me a big ripe paw-paw."

On 5th October they loaded the boat. There was not much, and most of it was for David's navigation: the chart graved in the plank, the sextant, the compass, the Nautical Almanac. The last was in a box with the men's letters and the captain's log, a log he had kept faithfully throughout their long three months on Minerva. They took ten tentacles of octopus each about nine inches in length, and a piece of shark for food.

Young Finau Laione was perturbed by the paucity of their rations; he felt that they should have more, for the men on the reef had the still and could fend for themselves for food. Though the *Malolelei* crew took a fishing-line for trolling it was unlikely that it would catch any fish, for they were traversing no shallow water, no reefs from which the fish would rise.

Since David mistrusted the rudder gudgeons he shipped also a fourteen-foot plank roughly shaped with the cane-knife to the semblance of a steering-oar; and a length of iron to nail opposite the mooring cleat to make a socket for the oar to work in, as though the cleat and the iron were thole-pins.

He had no means of measuring time; he would have to navigate on latitudes only, and what dead reckoning he could guess at. Knowing his direction, guessing the set, finding the latitude achieved and checking speed and direction against that, he could make an intelligent estimate of longitude too, especially since his course was so close to a northerly one; had it been east or west he would have been much more in the dark.

David spoke privately with the mate for a long time that night, leaving final instructions. Just what these were in their entirety none of the others ever knew; but they included the action the mate was to take if rescue did not come within a certain period and all hope was gone.

David addressed the men, at a prayer meeting. He said, "I leave all my responsibility to Ve'etutu. You have to do whatever he orders." He told them that on his voyage he would not be committed to a single destination, for he might have to change his plans with the wind and the circumstances. He urged them to keep up their prayers, with the beginning and the end of every day.

In the afternoon of the following day, Saturday, at 4 p.m., they left on their voyage, the captain and David Uaisele and Sateki. They had missed the high tide in the morning and they thought it necessary to wait for night, though there was in fact a good deep-water passage breaking the north-eastern chain of the western lagoon of the reef by which they were enclosed. They ran down there by evening and let go their anchor outside the reef in a good sheltered roadstead which Captain Denham, in the year 1854, had named Herald Bight. At fifteen fathoms it was the only anchorage in those seas; a few yards farther out from the reef the depths are still unplumbed.

At seven in the morning, Sunday, 7th October, they set their sails and moved off slowly to the northward.

The condition of the men left to the mate was this:

He had two men bedridden and very weak; they were William Fa, who was now stricken with the polyneuritis that had felled Fine Feuiaki, and Fine himself. He had two others who were ill and weak, but able to walk; they were Finau Laione, who was the thinnest of them all, and Fetaiaki Pulu, Soakai's son. Fetaiaki had spent a great many days lying in his bunk; some of the others, who felt fairly miserable themselves, believed he could have made a greater effort, and blamed his father Soakai for not driving him to it. But at the send-off for *Malolelei* he had been lively; he had actually been swimming round the boat, and seemed to have rallied from his weak condition.

154

Ve'etutu himself was in fine fettle; and others on whom he could depend for an effort were Talo Fifita, Sipa Fine, Vaiangina, Soakai, Saia Peni, and Teiapa'a Bloomfield. Saia had developed a bad backache over the past few weeks, but he didn't get much sympathy, for most of the others, in their impatience with him, thought it had the same origin as his earlier spells of fainting sickness, in which they could not quite believe.

Ve'etutu's first action was to order the distilling of water to take place every second day, day and night; twenty-four hours on and twenty-four hours off, for he believed he could get a more efficient supply this way instead of heating the great drum from cold every day. It was unlikely that they could keep up the fuel supply for more than this; wood was now very difficult to get, and his best men, Soakai and Sipa and Talo, had used most of their strength ripping off planks for the *Malolelei*.

Soakai's great burst of energy, which had earned him the admiration of most of his fellows, had come to an end. He was listless, and not capable of doing much fishing.

Ve'etutu also instituted another practice. Every day when the tide fell he made everyone capable of movement go for a walk, even though they might not be able to go far; and the walk seemed to encourage them. But he had to fight against a mental lassitude greater than David had encountered. There was, it is true, a greater hope pervading the small community after David sailed; but there was a greater loneliness too; the reef had always seemed lonely, but now it closed in on them.

"We missed David's leadership," Ve'etutu has said. "David was the best hand amongst us, and the best hope. We had the utmost faith in his ability and his resource. He was one of the coolest men I have ever seen, and his orders were always easily acceptable, at least at most times. Before he went he left most of the things to my decision; for example, I used to decide what each man should do each day. David would only intervene when he wanted something done another way, or when there was something new he wanted to institute.

"What have I learnt from Minerva Reef? I've thought of that often, because you should learn something from an experience. I have found out that there is something called responsibility, and that it means a very great deal. I felt that I had responsibility laid on me there; and what's more, I felt that I lived up to it. I felt closer to God there, and I still do—I *came* closer to God. I never before had the habit of praying; I have it now and I think I will always have it.

"Yes, I learnt a great deal on Minerva Reef. I feel I should be able, henceforth, always to carry out to the full my duties as captain, if I should get another ship. I feel as though I have qualified in a high-grade university."

That Sunday, after a prayer meeting in which Ve'etutu preached the sermon, he and Teiapa'a and Vaiangina went fishing and brought back sixteen octopus, nineteen crays and twenty-one fish. They sun-dried some clams and hung them up with some bêche-de-mer to augment their emergency supplies of food. In the evening Vaiangina preached a sermon on the subject of the Israelites being delivered from Egyptian bondage. He was a frequent preacher, though the only other Mormon in the group was Sipa Fine. "On the reef all men forgot they belonged to different churches," he says.

In the morning Talo and Finau Laione distilled the water. Soakai, Saia, and Teiapa'a broke out timber for the fire. Ve'etutu and Vaiangina went fishing and returned with eight octopus, fourteen fish and twenty shellfish of one sort or another. They shared them all round, and shared too their regular ration of water, ten ounces for the healthy and fourteen for the sick. Vaiangina conducted morning prayer, Ve'etutu the evening service.

On Wednesday the weather was rough, and Ve'etutu the only one able to go fishing. His catch was almost as great as when he was accompanied: thirteen octopus, eight fish, twenty-nine shellfish. They had the same water ration, and Soakai, Talo, Saia, and Teiapa'a broke the timber for the fire. Fine and William distilled the water. Fine was a little better; besides, they did not need to use their legs much just for watching the still.

This was the pattern of their days until Saturday, 13th October; but by Saturday a subtle change had come over them. Most of them had been thinking of the little *Malolelei*. If she were ever to make port it would be, they estimated, on this weekend. Perhaps some of them remembered the captain's prediction that if anything were to happen it would happen on a Tuesday. This would give time, in their estimation, for a rescue boat to arrive if David Fifita reported their predicament on the weekend.

The other omens were good, too. Fine Feuiaki was dreaming a lot. At times he used to dream that he was talking to his father, who had long been dead; at other times he used to dream of funerals. In the Tongan belief these are fortunate dreams, forecasting some happy event.

Perhaps it was this that made them use whatever was available for their fire: old lengths of rubber belting, rubber hose, fishing-lines, anything that would burn.

Ve'etutu went fishing with Fine and Teiapa'a. They caught fourteen octopus, twenty-eight shellfish, nine fish; and shared out the fish and the shellfish among the sick men, reserving the tougher, less attractive octopus for the healthy.

So it went on. On Sunday they didn't fish; but they kept up the distillation of water. In spite of Ve'etutu's early resolve, they had done this every day instead of every second day. On Monday, Ve'etutu was the only one fishing again. Fine and Teiapa'a distilled the water. This time they had only seven ounces for the healthy men, a little more for the sick. In the evening, just as the sun went down, Fetaiaki Pulu died.

Just before this, Ve'etutu apparently had a thought that it was about to happen. He came to William, where William was lying down, and said that Fetaiaki couldn't hang on to life; he begged William to cling to life with all that he knew, for help was coming. And so, when Fetaiaki died, it strengthened William Fa's desire to live.

Soakai was beside himself with grief. He had nourished the hope that his son was getting better, particularly after the efforts Fetaiaki had made at the launching of *Malole-lei*. In his resentment of fate he even accused Talo Fifita of causing the death, remembering that Talo had been at the wheel when they hit the reef. It was an unfortunate choice of scapegoat; for Talo, above all the others, held death in dread, and did not lightly forget or forgive the accusations.

The men held a prayer meeting beside the body; and afterwards they discussed what they must do with it.

Ve'etutu said, "We'll do nothing. We'll keep Fetaiaki with us here. Because I believe the *Malolelei* must by now have reached a destination."

And that was their decision. If a rescue ship should arrive they would ask the rescuers to take the body too. If that was impossible, so said the doughty mate, they'd leave the body in the wreck on the reef, and he'd get a boat somehow and come back for it.

"After tomorrow or the next day we'll know whether any hope is left and then we'll come to another decision," he said.

Soakai agreed.

They put the body alongside the fire, and Soakai sat with

his son, keeping his vigil through the night. Ve'etutu waited with him a little while, and then said he'd go to sleep, because of the fishing in the morning. He didn't sleep well. Their condition had deteriorated through the week, and only Teiapa'a and Vaiangina could still help him with the fishing. He had talked late, and, in the habit of fitness he had cultivated, it was his fashion to sleep more or less at will, but on this night he couldn't. He was lying with his head on his arm and his arm on the boards that had been a wall and were now a floor, when he heard a droning. When he lifted his head to listen he could no longer hear anything. He put his head down and he could hear it again.

The ship was acting as a sounding-board, and, realizing this, he thought the sound must have been coming from the sea or the air. He tried again, and this time when he lifted his head he could still hear the drone, but more faintly. He jumped up and climbed out on top of the ship. As he did so there was a cry from Vaiangina on watch. He too had heard the sound.

Ve'etutu shouted, "Vakapuna, Tamaiiki; Vakapuna!"—"Boys, wake up, it is an aeroplane!"—and now that they were all awake they could hear it all right, and Ve'etutu by this time could see it. He could see a red light and a green, and knew, therefore, that it was coming straight for them.

"Thank God!" he cried. "For David has reached land!"

Everyone was on top, or nearly everyone, shouting and waving and thanking God.

Ve'etutu shouted to them to bring the fire up; to show flames, to show the rescuers that they were still alive.

Sipa Fine leapt down to where the fire was burning and seized a brand flaming at one end. He jumped up through the hatch to bring this to the upper deck, and was in such a hurry that when he had his head and shoulders through the hatch he forgot he was carrying this in his hand; he hit it

159

sharply on the underside of the deck, and lost it all, spreading the embers everywhere.

Teiapa'a came up behind him with another brand; others came running with paper, rubber hose, anything that would make a fire and quickly. In their haste and their anxiety they were producing very little in the way of flame. They were laughing, and crying, and thanking God for His mercy, and getting in one another's way.

But while they fumbled, the aircraft dropped a candelabra flare and the night became as bright as day. The plane was low; they recognized it as one of the big flying-boats from Fiji; they could see the Air Force roundels.

It circled, a wide circle close to the sea, and came again into its own evocation of light, and dropped another kind of flare close against the Japanese ship, a little to the south and about thirty yards from it. Then another one to the north. These lights continued to burn, and the flying-boat circled again. This time a canister of food came down, swinging beneath a parachute, and it landed in a foot of water, no more, between the flares. It was low tide; on that day the low tide came at noon and midnight.

Ve'etutu sent two men to go and get the canister. They couldn't lift it, in their weakness and their excitement. He sent all who were fit, and they brought it to the little beach of sand below the wreck. The flying-boat went off, with a waggle of its wings, and then everyone was in the sea.

Ve'etutu assumed command and kept a strict control. He ordered the 'chute untied and put to one side. Then he ordered a stock-taking, to see what they had before anyone should eat. It was treasure.

There were ten tins of corned beef, five tins of vegetable and meat stew, five tins of sausage, ten tins of water, three tins of butter, four tins of milk, two tins of fish, six loaves of bread, and two can-openers. And there was a note which read: BOAT COMING.

Before they touched anything Ve'etutu called for attention and he prayed:

"Oh God our Father we thank Thee tonight for the help we have got. We thank Thee for keeping us from the days gone, in which we were in the mouth of Death. We thank Thee for giving us the food. We are in a place good for fish and for shellfish; but not for men to live in. We know that everything has been done from Thee. We are about to die but for your kindness in leading David Fifita to safety, through that to save us. We believe it all came from Thee. Our hope is still in Thee. We say thanks in the name of Jesus Christ. Amen."

Then he separated out the rations in equal shares. They reasoned that, since their position was now known, they would keep nothing in reserve for the following day.

They shared the water first; they had a tin of water each. By this time the event was turned into a picnic; the moon was at the full and their spirits at a peak. The water tins were empty in a moment; they replenished them with their milk ration.

The next thing they were hungry for was the bread, and the butter to go with it; and after that there was the meat.

"I was surprised when I counted them sitting round," Ve'etutu said later. "Some of them had been bedridden for weeks, but here was a full count. I told them it was good to see them all sitting in the circle. An hour or two before I had doubted whether William Fa could live till morning, and I was surprised to see him sitting there."

Hardly more surprised than William Fa himself. He had lost the use of his legs altogether, and he had come down the precipitous face of the wreck, from deck-beam to deck-beam, using his arms only, in a panic lest he miss the food and the water and the joy of the company entering into a new life.

When they had all eaten they had another prayer meeting, and this time it was a prayer of thanksgiving. They remembered that David had told them: "The first thing you will see will be a plane or a warship; by that you will know that I have arrived in Fiji."

They talked for an hour. Again they had a prayer meeting. They were kissing each other, hugging each other, shaking hands, trying to find some way to express their relief and their joy. They were boasting and making plans, saying what they would do when they got back to Tonga.

At four in the morning Ve'etutu told them to get back up into the wreck and try to sleep. If the rescue had to come from Tonga it might be a couple of days before the boat arrived, he said; there might be some difficulty that would hamper the rescue; and in fact they weren't out of the woods yet. Therefore, in the morning, they had to take up their programme of fishing again.

Some of them argued. They said no. The aircraft would arrive on the morrow and they would get another delivery of rations at least.

Ve'etutu repeated that all things were still uncertain, that there was still some danger. Then each man went to his own sleeping-place. William Fa dragged himself, on hands and elbows, as far as the ship. From there he had to be lifted up to the space they called a cabin. They all went to their beds, but there was little sleep.

In the morning the sun was well up when they arose, and the tide was falling. As soon as he was able, Ve'etutu alone went down, and walked out on the reef, and collected some shellfish and began to eat them; and while he was eating he heard the flying-boat. He called out to the others, and the excitement mounted again to that high pitch it had reached on the previous evening. When Ve'etutu came hurrying back, splashing through the receding pools along the path made familiar in three months and more, the others

162

crowded out on deck, and all the shouting and waving of the previous night began again.

The aircraft came overhead and circled; they were taking photographs; and the crew of the plane waved and shouted too. Then it flew off to the westward, circled round, and glided in to a landing on the lagoon; landing towards the Japanese wreck, but coming to a stop a few hundred yards away, in safe anchorage.

Soakai went over to Ve'etutu and said, "Look here. They've flown all this way to get us, and the crew will be weary. Now it's up to us to swim towards the plane to save them trouble."

William Fa, who could hardly move, said, "Yes. Give me a lifebelt, and I'll swim."

Ve'etutu answered them both. "They've come to save us," he said, "and not to kill us off. That's what will happen if we try to swim. We will wait to see if they send out a dinghy. Even if they're not coming over to us we don't swim. Even if the plane prepares to leave again I'll stop anyone who tries to swim."

Though their salvation waited there in front of them, in that bulky flying-boat that to their eyes looked as graceful as a gull, they could not quite believe it. Their minds raced round, in fear of what might happen to them yet before they came to safety; not even the sight of their vehicle convinced them that their ordeal was really over.

But then they saw a door open in the side of the aircraft and a rubber dinghy with an outboard motor being launched. It started to approach them. They were all laughing again, clapping hands, acting like madmen.

There were five men in the dinghy: the pilot, the doctor, a Tongan interpreter, and two crewmen. The pilot introduced himself as the officer in charge, and Ve'etutu stepped forward.

"We've been waiting for you to come," he said.

163

Chapter Eleven

THE sounds of surf were lonely sounds. Without intensification they closed in after the departure of the *Malolelei*, and their never-ceasing reminder of waste and isolation was accentuated. The sounds were in their variety unalterable, except in times of storm, when small thunders became great, the sussurations of small surges of water were transformed into loud reverberating crashings of the driven masses, and the groanings and gurglings of the wash in the innumerable holes and passages and caverns of the coral became the bellowing of the Kraken.

Even the sea-bird's cry was almost alien here; the reef offered no shelter to most of the varieties of shore-birds that men associate with waters; the distance was too great for the ranging frigate-bird to travel there from any island that could serve him as a roost; the mollyhawks and albatrosses, the Cape Pigeons and the little stormy petrels, all the birds of open ocean that sleep upon the waters were not advantaged by the reef, and did not make a haunt of it.

And the men on the reef were conscious then of the proximity of death; three of their fellows were dead, and others were becoming resigned to death's approach. But if they were lonely, and afraid, their condition was infinitely preferable to that of the three men in the sailing-boat.

The *Malolelei*, that Sunday morning, waited at the anchorage at Herald Bight while David, for the last time, went over every item of their gear, the standing and running rigging, the fastenings, the mast, the rudder. He checked again his figures for the chart, using the degrees marked on the sextant to remeasure the angles. The sea was heavy, too heavy for his satisfaction; for while he trusted the ship to weather it, it offered too great a strain for men so physically ill-prepared as were he and his companions.

They would be racing against time, and they could not depend on any quality of speed; for *Malolelei* offered only sturdiness. Her planks were unavoidably too rough to slip through the water; her sails were not in any condition to be spread against a stiff blow; her bamboo mast had only the strength of its fishing-line stays to offer.

So about nine o'clock on that Sunday morning David knew he could wait no longer. Luck, that from the time of their leaving Nuku'alofa had been against him, was against him still; their anchor was jammed in the coral and they could not move it. The water on the anchorage was too deep to permit of diving; not all their strength, not all their manoeuvring of their vessel could shift it. They cut the anchor line and left the anchor behind.

It was a further limitation upon their capacity to survive; for they could think of a dozen situations in which the possession of an anchor might be sovereign. They might sight an island, for example, on a stormy night and be unable to stay in its lee; they might sight it in such a relationship to the wind that they could not approach it closer; but a spell on the anchor might give them an opportunity to wait for fishing canoes to come out. They could not know what lay ahead of them, and the anchor might make the difference between life and death. But they had no choice.

They hoisted the sails. David Uaisele took the tiller, and with David Fifita and his son Sateki sitting forward of him, their feet in the open hatchway, he put her close-hauled on a starboard reach and headed for the infinitely small fly-spot on the chart that was the island of Ono-i-Lau. Since it lay more than 200 miles to the northward, the course called for an accuracy in steering of one quarter of a degree. This was impossible, but holding to an accuracy of three or four degrees ought to put them eventually in a position from which, if the weather and the time of day were right, they would see the island, and have a fifty-fifty chance of making it.

Since Ono-i-Lau lay just to the east of due north from the South Minerva Reef, and since the wind had come from the east rather than from the south-east, as he desired, the captain had to make every foot of easting possible to him; the necessity slowed his already slow boat, and he could not average more than about two knots. In making this course they took a savage buffeting from the beam seas that came sweeping in from starboard. They were wet from the moment of setting out; they did not mind, for the heat of the sun was more oppressive to them, and the water and the wind were cooling; the glare of the sun, reflected a million times in the flying water, was a trial.

Ono-i-Lau is a group of six islands, but since they are encircled by a single reef they form a unit for mariners. Not only was this the nearest land, but since the cluster is of high islands, it stood the best chance of being seen.

In the first hour of their voyage David Fifita was busy, checking again, looking at all the gear under stress, making slight adjustments to the standing rigging. At the end of this time he relieved Uaisele at the tiller; and at that moment a particularly large sea ripped the rudder away, demonstrating the weakness David had feared. They had gone only two or three miles on their voyage. They dropped the sails and, rocked and thrown about like spindrift, attached the steel bar they had brought for a thole-pin and got the steering-oar in place. It was a success, and they were on their way.

David took the helm all Sunday, and all through Sunday night, and the wind and the waves held exactly the same throughout that period. They were continuously drenched by the heavy seas, and in the night they were cold and shivering. They could keep nothing on deck, and while the hold gave them a shelter, it was a miserable place, with headroom of about eighteen inches. But the other two took turns trying to sleep there. And from time to time they prayed.

"That little boat I called *Malolelei* so that my father would perhaps intercede for us," David said later. "He would know all that we were suffering, because he drowned in the sea. And in *Malolelei* the three of us said the Rosary out loud. Why I was able to help the others, the men on the reef, so much was because God helped us, and Our Lady, and the saints helped, and that is what I believe. Now that I am safe, and also because I was not able to help them all but lost some of my men, I ask God to make me stronger, so that in future I can help people more than I have done."

The storm and the seas and the howling nightmare of wind continued until the Wednesday morning; and throughout that time the captain sat with the steering-oar and steered the boat. They tried to tell time by the height of the sun, and the positions of the stars and the moon; and the captain relinquished the steering-oar only in the brief moments when he used the sextant to try and find a latitude. On Wednesday morning the wind dropped a little; the seas no longer washed over them, and David asked Uaisele to relieve him while he changed his clothes.

167

He had lost a great deal of weight; and he could not sit for very long in any position without suffering the severest pains. This applied to them all; even in their sleep if they occupied a position for half an hour their flesh protested, and the pains necessitated a change of attitude. Sometimes David steered sitting on the deck, sometimes squatting, sometimes lying full length. They adopted ridiculous attitudes, all of them, to ease the pain that came with inaction.

Such pain was aggravated always by their wet clothes. The clothes between the deck and their skin chafed them, the skin was raw and red in great patches, and the salt stung them. The sunshine on Wednesday and the quieter seas gave them a chance to strip off and hang their clothes to dry, and to get a little warm.

But by this Wednesday they had run out of food and water. The water had lasted them less than they thought. They had hoped that perhaps they might catch fish by trolling, and on Tuesday indeed they caught one; but it was a fish they did not recognize. They had never seen its like before and were frightened of poison, and so they threw it overboard. They had some of the ten tentacles of sundried octopus left; but between the sun and the sea-water it was rotting, and they could not eat it. They had finished the small fresh shark. There was no use in conserving such rations, for they would not keep.

Wednesday was the best day of all; it was almost an enjoyable day but for their pains, the pains of inaction and the pangs of hunger. But they hoped to raise the island of Ono-i-Lau on Thursday; this kept them in spirits; this and their prayers and their faith.

On Thursday the weather continued good. The captain, steering still, saw a bird circling him, and watched it. Two or three times it went over, following above him, its sharp little head looking down on him. It would ease up from his port quarter, hover in the air above him, wheel away.

David watched and watched, and hoped it would alight.

When it did, it perched upon the steering-oar, behind him. He called to Uaisele, who was nearest, warning him to move gently. He told him to make no move until he was ready; the bird was on the oar and, as near as David could judge, was close behind his elbow. Uaisele could not see the bird; David told him to move up gently, keeping David between him and his quarry; to move up close to David, and suddenly to reach over his neck and grasp the bird at first sight.

Uaisele followed instructions, and in the necessities of near-starvation played his part perfectly. He thrust forward over David's shoulder and caught the bird, and the three of them shouted for joy. They cut through the neck and squeezed its blood into a little plastic cup; they crushed the little body to extract every drop of blood, and it filled the cup a little more than halfway, perhaps about three ounces. To this they added the spirit from the compass; the red liquid nearly filled the cup.

The little draught was shared by Sateki and Uaisele, David refusing. It gave them a small respite from their cravings. Then they separated the bird, cut it in sections, and chewed on the raw flesh.

Though David had insisted on taking the smallest share of water while they were on Minerva Reef, this might have been construed as a gesture; and in fact David himself described the action as a calculated one, designed to contribute to the respect in which the men held him, and thus shore up his authority. But when he shared the sea-bird's blood amongst the others no such motive existed. His authority was complete, for of his companions one was his son and the other his physical inferior; both of them were dependent upon his knowledge and his ability for their safety, and both of them were almost fanatically loyal to him. His sacrifice therefore reflected his integrity; he put

169

his own needs last and had no other motive. So this action indicated that his behaviour on Minerva in all probability stemmed entirely from an unselfish consideration for others.

David believed by this time that they should be in the latitude of Ono-i-Lau, and as midday approached he prepared to take a shot of the sun. To his disappointment they had not made the distance he expected; as nearly as he could judge, their latitude was still well south of the island.

In the afternoon he took over the helm again, and stayed there without a break until nine o'clock next morning. At 3 a.m. Uaisele, sitting forward, reported seeing a light far off to port; and when the others had seen it they guessed it to come from a fishing vessel. They changed course, sailing down wind, hoping to intercept it, but it seemed to draw away from them. They followed on, nevertheless; until in an hour or so they saw another light to the northward, back on their original course. They turned to that; but it, too, seemed to draw away. Then far to the south they saw a third light, and it seemed to be overtaking them. They held their course, hoping, their hearts high; but then the dawn began to lighten the east, and after a little while the lights disappeared altogether; and it was no more than a mystery they could not solve.

At nine in the morning David's breathing was becoming difficult; he called Uaisele to relieve him. At noon he took more shots of the sun; and going over all his calculations he became convinced that they were to the east of the island; they therefore changed course a little to run on a more westerly direction. This increased their speed slightly; the wind was still an easterly and it had freshened throughout Thursday night and Friday, so again they were being soaked with flying spray and the water splashing from the outrigger. They had to run again on the jib alone; they were not certain of their rigging, and for them, with so little time to accomplish their journey before they died, a sailing mishap would certainly mean disaster.

Running in the darkness that night, they believe they saw the island, a mass on the clouded horizon; but it lay to the north-east of them; they had probably overshot it while sailing too far to the south. They were afraid of Ono-i-Lau, particularly in the dark; there are mighty reefs about the island that could have brought them then to quick disaster; and in any case they could not now beat back against the wind.

But the confirmation of an approximate position heartened David; it meant that they were approaching the vast complex of islands that is Fiji, and it was a promise that they would soon strike land. He made a course for the next of several possible destinations: the island of Matuku.

This is a volcanic island in the Moala group, eleven square miles in extent and, for most small craft, only a night's sail from the Fijian capital of Suva. It has an anchorage on its western coast, but no safe harbours; and again this worried David Fifita; for, if they should strike a reef, he did not know that they would have the strength to survive.

When they were at their prayers he spoke to his companions and again impressed upon them that, while it was not important that all should live, it was essential for the eleven living men on Minerva that one of the three of them should reach safety. The deterioration in their physical condition, now painfully apparent, was worrying; but he impressed upon them that if one should survive, any one of them, their mission was accomplished.

From 10 o'clock that Friday night until midnight Saturday they held their new course; they were making better time, but the destination again worried him. At midnight Saturday he changed course again, and this time headed frankly west, for the island of Kandavu. He could be reasonably sure of a landfall, for Kandavu is a large island, about thirty miles long, and varying in breadth from a quarter to eight miles. It is generally the first land seen by travellers approaching the Fijis from the south, and its north coast is only about five miles from Suva.

With the majority of its outliers, it is a volcanic island with high mountains, rising to 2,700 feet above the sea, and it possesses a large number of sheltered bays and harbours. It has a population of about 8,000, practically all of them Fijians.

But no one has seen the landfall of its ragged mountain range with more joy than the *Malolelei* crew, as they approached it from the east in the first light of dawn. The island was life to them and to their fellows, but between them and that life lay the barrier of the Great Astrolabe Reef, which, on the eastern side of Kandavu and its immediately associated islets, has few breaks.

David and his crew picked up the break of the sea in the dark. At about the point where they came in contact the reef runs from east to west, under the eastern bend of the island; and is almost unbroken. They hauled down the mainsail here, and crept along under the jib, a few yards out from the breakers on the reef, looking for a passage they could negotiate.

The sea was still heavy, the wind still racing in from the east, so that there was a chop even beyond the reef. They looked for signs of life, fishing canoes or schooners on the ocean, but there was nothing. They followed the reef a distance of ten miles or more without finding a passage. An exceptionally heavy surf was raised in two or three places where the reef reached to the southward; but with the wind behind them the men had full control, and easily evaded any of the dangers.

They were buoyed with hope, and the frustration of being fenced from the land scarcely dampened their spirits; though in places the true coast lay only a quarter or half a mile beyond the savage coral ramparts. When an opening appeared the chance came suddenly; and David swung the long steering-oar to put *Malolelei* again on a starboard tack; reaching up into an opening no wider than 300 yards.

While this was an ample channel under normal conditions, the height of the seas that had been raised by more than a week of steady wind made it a danger-spot; they lifted up here from either side, and were funnelled by the shape of the reefs into a crest.

The opening breached the barrier that otherwise stretched from side to side across the mouth of Soso Bay. It was especially dangerous, because the deep running current which kept the opening free turned immediately back towards the east, inside the reef; and this, for *Malolelei*, was the impossible direction. Dead ahead of the opening, the water, which elsewhere in the vicinity was from seventeen to thirty fathoms deep, shallowed up to three or four. The enormous breakers, already peaked up by the funnelling of the channel on the ocean side, were raised to a steep, precipitous angle by this shallowing; and, before David or his companions could appreciate the danger, the *Malolelei* was picked up bodily and thrown off the crest of the wave, a crest which David estimates, with a typical lack of exaggeration, to have been at least sixteen feet high.

She was flung in such a way that her starboard quarter somersaulted over her port bow. The only part of the ship that touched was the mast, which broke off on the shallowing bank. Sturdy construction left *Malolelei* floating upside-down, but otherwise undamaged.

When the wave tailed out, David was clinging to *Malolelei*; the other two had been thrown clear, and were thirty yards inshore. He called for them to come back to the ship, and they tried, but they were making no headway against the strong tide pouring through the gap in the reef; and they were protesting, too; they wanted to swim ashore. David himself was not convinced that they could do anything with *Malolelei* if they returned; she could not have been put back on her keel, and there was no way of knowing how long they would have to drift with her. David began to swim landward, towards the others.

Early that morning they had been battered by a squall; they had put their lifebelts on at that time, and had retained them as they encountered the reef.

From the point of their capsize the land was more distant than it had been from any other part of the reef they had negotiated. The nearest part was a cape which ran out, contiguous to the reef, and perhaps a mile and a quarter or a mile and a half back towards the east. Initially the current was running in this direction, and it was to this point that they began to make their way. For a time all went well. But the long ordeal they had been through was against any sustained effort; they could not keep up the steady, disciplined kind of swim that was their only hope; at least Sateki could not, and he was by far the best swimmer of the three.

He fell behind, and David saw him discard his lifebelt. He swam back and told him to put it on. Sateki complained that it interfered with his swimming; he could make no headway while he was wearing it. David insisted that he wear it; and under these orders Sateki put it on again. They turned again towards the shore, and had made considerable progress, when Sateki again fell back.

He was in the last stages of exhaustion, and David turned back to him once more. Sateki insisted he could make a better effort without the bulk of the life-jacket impeding his progress; and since his situation, and the situation of them all was desperate, David allowed the boy to use his judgment.

But he thought the life-jacket might yet be necessary. He tried to wear it himself over his own, to adjust the straps so that he could wear them both. It was not a success, and for a time he swam towing the additional life-belt. But still Sateki fell behind, unencumbered as he was; and again his father turned back to him, discarding the spare lifebelt as he did so.

But as he came close to his son this time his heart failed him, for the boy was taking in water at the mouth. They had covered more than a mile of the distance to the shore; more than two-thirds of the total distance; but there seemed no hope that Sateki could go farther. David swam to him and held him up, and tried to give him encouragement; but Sateki seemed to have lost the power of understanding. The long hard effort had been too much for him; if he still swam he swam as an automaton.

As David waited there with him he saw something that filled him with an even greater dismay; for David Uaisele, whom he had seen within a short swimming distance of the shore, had now turned, and was coming back to the assistance of them both. In this lay total destruction, for if one of them did not get ashore the men on South Minerva had to die.

David shouted to Uaisele, but this was useless; the swimmer kept coming back to them; and he knew that he must abandon his son. But first he held him close, for in this, as in every other moment of stress in a life that had been far from calm, he turned to his God. He held Sateki while he said a short prayer:

"Jesus, Mary and Joseph. I give you my heart and my soul. Jesus, Mary and Joseph, help me in the last moments of my life. Jesus, Mary and Joseph, I place all my trust in you. Amen."

When that was said he pushed the lad gently away, and turned to swim to Uaisele. When Uaisele saw him coming he paused, treading water. He too was near the end of his strength; but this time when David shouted he went ahead of him towards the land. But they had come to a place where the easterly wind was slapping the waves in his face, and a tide was keeping him from his destination, and he stopped again. David shouted to him to turn north, and head towards an island that was, perhaps, a full half-mile away, perhaps a little more; and when Uaisele did that he found the going a little easier.

At this point David looked back. Sateki was still on the surface, and he was swimming, but swimming aimlessly, going round in circles, with actions that could not hold him in his place for long.

David followed Uaisele, and noted that he too was failing, though they had come to calmer water now; he was resting every few strokes, and sinking back; and after a while he stopped trying and rested altogether. David came up close to him and spoke to him; but Uaisele made no effort. Then David shouted angrily, but since that also had no effect he kicked Uaisele savagely in the side; and with that the carpenter gathered himself together, and began to swim towards the island.

He went about fifty yards and stopped again. While he swam he swam more quickly and efficiently than David; but he was at the end of effort. The fifty yards were all he could accomplish; and again David swam up to him; and Uaisele looked at him with dull eyes.

David swore at him, told him to remember the men on the reef, told him to swim. Uaisele made no effort; made no effort, either, as David realized with a shock, to stop the water that was slopping in at his mouth.

So David swam up close, and lifted himself high in the water, and swung his arm with all the strength he could muster, and hit Uaisele across the jaw and the ear; hit him hard and cursed him, and hit him again, and got a dawning recognition; and Uaisele set off again.

They had about 300 yards to go to the small island, an

island called Nmbia; and now it was the nearest land, and their only hope. Uaisele swam only fifty yards again, and stopped for the third time; and again David went to drive him on, as a man drives a dumb beast with blows and invective; but before he reached him he stopped; for Uaisele's feet had found, by accident, and by the first luck that had attended them, the top of a niggerhead, a pillar of coral reaching towards the surface from the depths; and he could stand. He stood and rested there, gaining his breath, up to his neck in water; and, since he could see the shadow of another head of coral in the vicinity, David swam to it, and rested his feet on it. His head was also above water, and there they waited.

Now they could look back to where they had left Sateki; but there was nothing, only the rippled water, nothing to show that a man had died there, a man who was their better in the sea. They stood on their niggerheads and regained some of their strength; and saw other pillars of coral ahead of them, and so swam from one to the next, a few poor strokes at a time, one man following the other, until at last, a hundred yards from shore, their feet touched bottom and they walked.

It would be more true to say of them at this stage that they dragged themselves; they were not men, but aching muscle; they knew nothing except the relief from an ordeal which their minds refused to encompass. They came to the island at last and threw themselves on the ground; they lay on the shingle in the last stages of life, and saw above their heads the fronds of a coconut, a crown of leaves girding the clusters of green and golden fruit.

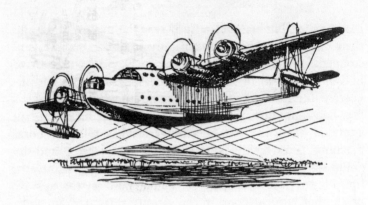

Chapter Twelve

THE day was overcast, and though they were sheltered from the wind by the protruding cape, they lay cold and shivering upon their island; their strength taxed to its ultimate contribution, and their minds swamped and beaten down by the inundations of the realization of safety.

They had been, as close as they could estimate, more than two hours in the water, and this physical effort came at the end of one hundred days of privation which had starved their bodies of certain essentials. They were distraught, too, by the loss of their companion Sateki, David's eldest and best-loved son; and the circumstances in which he had gone, swimming at their sides one moment and the next for ever lost to them, made sorrow more acute. Then, and for many days thereafter, it was an agony for David.

A returning acuity of consciousness was assisted by the entry of familiar smells and sounds; the penetrating odour of growth enveloped them, the shrill voices of birds, whistling and crying, the beat of wings. The shrills of grasshoppers and frogs separated themselves one at a time from a chorus they had forgotten existed. The chatter of crickets was insistent; and from all of these loved sounds they had been long divorced.

And when they lifted their heads the colour flooded in upon them, the brilliant sunny green of Fiji, the dark green shadows flecked with the brilliance of flowers—of red ginger and reed orchids and hibiscus. The blue heron quietly fishing was a wonder in their vision, and the squawking parrot in the palm fronds. Even the smell of swamp mud was sweet; there had been no mud on South Minerva. Even the grey of the palm trunk was something to see and ponder on; the jewels of dragonflies were rich reward. But it was the smell of damp growth that was nectar; the smell of growing things nourished by fresh sweet water. Through their senses the world came back to them, and encouraged them to make themselves one with it again. The sun tempered their shivering, and seemed to give them hope.

It was not enough to remove their mental chill; and they could have lain there, both of them, until the pain of thinking was eliminated by unconsciousness and death; but their duty was to others; their task was not yet done.

Somewhere they had to find other people, and tell them of the eleven weary shipwrecked men who waited on a half-tide reef 300 miles to the south and east.

They could go no farther, though, without refreshment; and the palm offered it to them. Luckily for their frame of mind it was not tall, as coco-palms are estimated; its crown with the nuts was not much more than twenty feet from the ground, and Uaisele believed that he could climb it.

"I haven't climbed a palm for four years," he said to David, and the inconsequential remark somehow seemed to lessen the enormity of the task. For when he was a boy, Uaisele, like most islanders, could climb a palm in seconds. When he approached this one, weak and staggering, he could hardly summon up the strength to place his feet

179

upon the butt of it. He stood there, holding the trunk with both hands, and looking towards the prize of nuts among the stems. Do what he could, he was unable to get his feet to travel upwards.

So he tried another way, gripping the trunk with his thighs, grasping with his hands, his thighs and his ankles, shifting the weight from thighs to ankles and back again, each time making an inch or two towards the top. It took him fifteen minutes to climb the twenty feet and accomplish the miracle. When he reached the top he threw down nine green nuts, good nuts, full of liquid. They drove a stake into the sand and husked the nuts and drank them.

There must have been an average of twenty to thirty ounces in each nut; one is sufficient, and sometimes too much, for a thirsty man; but they kept husking and drinking. David was sick; he vomited when the liquid began to fill his stomach, and thus he drank a little more than Uaisele, but the thirst of neither man was quenched; they stopped drinking because they had finished the nuts, and there was no other palm near by; and for a little while at least Uaisele did not have the strength to climb again. Anyway the reward would not have been the same, for he had thrown down all the nuts worth drinking.

The next task that faced them was the crossing of the channel that separated this small island from Kandavu. The distance was no more than a quarter-mile; they entered the water and began to walk. At the deepest part it came no higher than their necks; they did not have to swim and they made the shore without mishap.

Consciously or unconsciously they had headed towards a point where two more coco-palms grew; Uaisele climbed them both, and from each of them he threw down more nuts. Besides the green drinking nuts he threw down a ripe one, to give them something to eat. They were now on solid land where people lived; but they still had a long way to go and they did not know in which direction. Then as they were husking the nuts they saw, nearly two miles along the beach to their right, a single house.

They decided to go that way. Luck was not yet on their side, having deserted them from the moment they left Tonga; for there were habitations at fairly close hand in the opposite direction; but they could not know this. They knew that the beach at this point was a soft muck; they had sunk to their knees coming ashore; and they hesitated again before they tackled it.

Nor was this imagined ordeal lightened in any way in the actuality. The muck of the beach continued soft; where it ended, furthest from the water, the sharp rocks began and the cliff grew out of them. There was no way for the two men to avoid the clinging ooze that made every step heavy; but they struggled on for a mile and a half, more than three thousand yards, more than four thousand separate and individual efforts to pull a foot from the mud and forge ahead.

The house was still in front of them, a long way away, when they came to a place where a man had been walking on the beach that morning. His track led off, up the hill to the right, and they followed it, hoping to strike a path. There was indeed a path, and at the place where it met the beach a coco-palm grew; a tall palm, sixty or more feet high; and once again Uaisele prepared himself to climb.

Somehow he accomplished it, and they husked the nuts and drank. In that morning they had, between them, drunk twenty-nine nuts and eaten the meat of a ripe one; but at each drinking David had vomited most of it up again; he could not keep the sustenance in his stomach. Uaisele had retained it all; his belly was distended with what he had drunk.

When they had rested again, they followed the path; a

single track, not much used; and it brought them out, at the top of the hill, to a wider one that looked as though it were, perhaps, a thoroughfare between two villages. They could not decide which way to go; and while they stood wondering they heard the sound of a *lali*, the wooden drum which in Fiji calls villagers to their church.

At that they looked themselves over. Each man was wearing a cotton singlet, and on top of that his lifebelt; for now their lifebelts were all they owned. They were determined to keep them with them; and wearing them was the easiest way to carry them. The kapok-filled canvas, wet though it was, had acquired some warmth from their bodies; they were still cold and shivering and appreciated this slight protection. Uaisele's singlet had shrunk; it hardly came below his waist; David's was well down on his thighs.

It was a remarkable time to think of modesty, but they did; and Uaisele gathered from beside the road some leaves of banana and draped them about his middle. Then they walked down the track in the direction of the sound.

A little farther along they came to a house sitting in its plantation, and from it came the sound of voices. They did not approach, but sheltered behind some tapioca bushes in the garden, that hid them up to their waists. When they felt they were sufficiently concealed David called out; he speaks Fijian excellently, though it is a tongue quite alien to his own.

A woman came out of the house and looked at him and Uaisele, the two men half-hiding behind the tapioca, and David called again.

"Is there a man in the house?" he asked.

She went back inside, and in a moment a man named Taniela Delai came to them, and they had made their contact with the world.

Delai took them immediately to the house, saw them stripped of their clothes and made warm, and fed them on taro, which in Fiji is called "dalo", and on "lu", the cooked green leaves of taro.

He said later that he had such a fright, seeing the two men heavily bearded, with their hair long to their shoulders, dressed in singlets and lifebelts, haggard and wild, that he nearly ran away.

By this time the afternoon was wearing away. It was 3.30; and their effort of swimming two miles and walking four had taken them ten hours.

A Fiji village is still today, as it has been throughout the history that Fijians remember, a communal undertaking. Some modifications have been introduced with civilization; but still, in most villages, particularly on outlying islands, the crops are communally owned.

Houses, built of the materials at hand, are erected by all the men of the village for a private occupation; and replacement and repair of houses is a village affair. All the men of the village have their duties, looking after the crops, attending to the entertainment of visitors, mending the paths and roadways; and they take their orders from a local headman, the *turaga-ni-koro*, the administrative head of the village.

Each district or group of villages is administered by a higher official, the *Buli*; and he can order certain work to be performed by a village or a group of villages. There is, in effect, no private ownership; though a man's possession of a communally owned house is complete. Within it he is his own master, and he can, if he so wishes, close its doors to others. In that climate these hospitable people seldom do.

There has been a recent tendency to break away from this ancient system. As civilization brings new trades and skills, and as the young are educated to new ways of thought, some dissatisfaction has been expressed. The pride of private ownership is beginning to influence those who have not yet achieved such a thing; and village thought now concedes the privilege to certain people who may, for one reason or another, prosper better outside the system.

Taniela Delai was such a man, "exempt from communal duties", as the official Fijian phrase goes. He had built his house and cleared his garden patch away from the boundaries of the village, and he owed it no more than the normal duties of citizenship as these are reckoned anywhere. The Fijian finds a decision to sever village ties a difficult one to make in spite of the more obvious advantages; it is a break with tradition and with the kinship ties the village represents; but it is becoming more and more common. Nevertheless the independent cropper, like Taniela, retains a relationship with the village; and, as soon as he saw his guests from the sea were settled in comfort, Taniela ran to the village of Nacomotu to report.

Josiah Tokarua, the *turaga-ni-koro*, came with others to collect David and Uaisele, brought them into the village, and allotted a special *bure*, a Fijian house, to them. He detailed four men to light a fire to warm the house, and a number of women to tend to their physical comfort. The women applied hot presses to the Tongans' flesh, anointed them with oil, and massaged them, kept them fed, and looked after them throughout the night.

In spite of their extreme exhaustion, David Fifita and David Uaisele both attended the evening church service in the village.

While this went on, the *turaga-ni-koro* sent a runner on foot to Vunisea, the main Kandavu settlement, with news of the two men. The runner returned at 5 a.m. on Monday. The first radio calls to Suva were made that morning; but the inadequate nature of the messages obscured the fact that assistance was urgently needed for the men on South Minerva; indeed, the name and location of the reef were not known, the men from the sea were not identified with the *Tuaikaepau,* and the only urgency was reckoned to be in providing succour for the two who had arrived.

At this stage David Fifita decided not to tell the story of their voyage, nor to identify himself and the other survivor; for in his pain and agony he wanted to be the first to tell Alapasita of their son's death.

A message had also been sent to the Buli Naceva, the administrative head of Naceva district; and he arrived in the morning at Nacomotu village. At nine the same morning a messenger in a small boat powered with an outboard motor came to take the two men to the main village, where there was a sergeant of police and a small hospital staffed with an assistant medical officer and four nurses.

David protested that they were too weak to be moved; a statement that was nothing less than the truth, and the first admission he had made that any task was beyond them. The reaction from their effort was setting in. But a result of this visit was that the position as to the other survivors of the *Tuaikaepau* was clarified; and that afternoon the first messages indicating the urgency of that situation were sent from Vunisea. They were acted upon almost at once by the commanding officer of the Royal New Zealand Air Force Station at Lauthala Bay in Suva.

On Monday night the sergeant of police came to Nacomotu village; and at two the next afternoon, Tuesday, the outboard took David and Uaisele round to the hospital.

Suva, on Monday afternoon, was still so ill-supplied with news of the event, and the spelling of the radio operator was so much at fault—not necessarily because of his personal deficiencies—that for a brief time the reef could not be identified; and no one knew where to look for the eleven men still thought to survive. Several suggestions were made, and charts were searched for a reef named "Manavu". But the Lauthala Bay squadron, on being notified, recognized the reef as Minerva and the situation as urgent.

A request was made that at first light on Tuesday a Sunderland should make a mercy flight to the reef. As it was already evening, that seemed reasonable; no landing could be made till next day. Group Captain J. D. Robins, who commanded the station, had other ideas.

"If we go tonight we may save a life," he said.

It is almost certain that the decision did indeed save the life of William Fa; by midnight the castaways had some relief from the extremities of their position. Before that, the Fiji Broadcasting Commission's radio station at Suva had released a short news item, and Tonga Radio, having caught the broadcast more or less by accident, had repeated it over its own station.

Tongan telephone wires were running hot as people sought confirmation, and news, more news. In the picture-show in Nuku'alofa the film was stopped and an announcement made. The excitement was intense, for *Tuaikaepau* had carried some of the best-known Tongans, and the presumed loss of seventeen men had been disastrous for the little country.

But on Monday there was no more news. The station could tell the public only that two men of three on a raft had survived, and that three at least of the remaining fourteen on the reef had died. Tonga Radio had monitored the Fiji Broadcasting Commission from the moment of the first announcement; and, with its local knowledge of the *Tuaikaepau* and her complement, was able to give a better coverage.

Having dropped supplies to the men on South Minerva, and having visually confirmed the existence of the castaways, and the fact that some were alive, the flying-boat returned to Fiji and was immediately prepared for another flight to rescue the men. This time it was commanded by Squadron Leader B. J. O'Connor, and carried a medical officer, Squadron Leader K. R. Bremner. A Tongan medical student from Fiji, Tupou Vaipulu, a health officer attached to the medical department in Suva, went along in case an interpreter should be needed. The Sunderland took off from Lauthala Bay shortly after 8 a.m., and arrived at South Minerva at noon.

It was a tragically pathetic-looking group they met there, a despondency of heavily bearded men; joyous for the moment, certainly, but bearing deep scars of suffering. They could have been cast appropriately for a Passion Play, except perhaps for young Finau Laione, who had not yet come by his beard. They were quiet and pathetically grateful; but they were too close to the sorrow and the ordeal; they spoke happily, but some could not speak at all.

Five of them were bedridden, unable to move much. Five were on their feet; and they told of Fetaiaki, who had died on the previous evening. In strong contrast to the rest of them was the leader, Ve'etutu Pahulu the mate. He was active and tried to help; he moved with assurance as though the reef were his natural home; he was still well muscled. He offered his services for every task; the rescuers were amazed at his energy and his obvious capacity for survival.

The castaways had a pathetic small cargo of mementoes to bring along with them. When he had sailed away, David Fifita, either in the superb confidence of making a successful voyage, or in the hope that he could instil such a confidence in the others, had left a list of articles he wanted rescued. Heading the list were the two remaining tubs of soya-bean sauce.

"Alapasita is very fond of it," he explained.

Then there was the engine casing he had used for a dish; the casing which, on one occasion, Talo had twice drained of fresh rainwater. There was the penicillin with its syringe, some sheets of the plastic they had used to make swim-goggles, the *sake* glass they had first used as a measure and the small tumbler that had replaced it; and a few other oddments. David had also insisted that the men carry their life-jackets, as they had done in their rescue drill; and, though they had to wear the life-jackets of the flying-boat, they had all obeyed him in this.

Finau Laione brought nothing for himself; he was pleased to have his life. Sipa Fine brought his training jacket with the hood; he had guarded it carefully all the time. He also had a serviceable speaker from the Japanese public-address system, though he was not quite sure what he would do with it. Talo Fifita had one just like it. William Fa had been too ill to bother with anything.

Vaiangina brought along one of the lamp-protectors he had used as a drinking-glass, and the bottle in which he had conserved his water ration; a small brown medicine bottle. None of them will ever forget the value of water; Sipa Fine, who never had dreams, and doesn't yet, can be brought to tears by the sight of a jug of clear water. Always close to his consciousness is the memory of the intensity of his thirst upon the reef, though with his companions he can laugh and joke about things that happened on South Minerva and might have been serious enough in their time: the look on the face of someone close to death, a ludicrous expression on someone else deprived moment-arily of food, a silly argument a couple of them had.

Nothing Soakai brought back compensated him for his losses on the reef; his son Fetaiaki, and that other boxer-son who was killed in a Tongan ring in the same week. Somewhere in the depths there lies, too, the belt he wore with pride as Tongan heavyweight champion; he regrets that. But he treasures the diary he kept carefully. There are gaps of weeks in it, when he was too busy or too exhausted to write; but what is written is a crystallization of many memories. His daughters have read it through and through; they know it by heart.

Teiapa'a Bloomfield brought the shell of the turtle he caught. It is a symbol for him; a symbol of a new kind of life he found on that southern waste; and his family guards it carefully. Ve'etutu brought the log-book he kept from the time of Fifita's departure from Minerva, a thin, blue-covered exercise book smelling strongly of fish—not a bad smell, but a definite and persistent one.

And a communal possession is their Bible; ragged, tattered, so worn and used that it is nearly impossible to tell the beginning from the end; the pages eaten away to a quarter of their depth, the paper brittle. Like the log-book, it smells of fish; but surely it will be a Tongan treasure as long as its further preservation is possible.

The rubber dinghy took the sick men out to the flying-boat first; and on its return journey to the Japanese wreck it brought a supply of water, and of a thick soup with potatoes and meat, and the ingredients of a good meal.

There were tasks for the airmen: the doctor had to check the grave of Fatai Efiafi; they investigated the living-quarters and marvelled at the still and the water supply. When the five men had fed, and while the men already in the aircraft were eating, they collected up the belongings, and wrapped the body of Fetaiaki in a blanket.

When the ten castaways were together in the plane, Vaiangina conducted a prayer meeting; they prayed together in joy and thankfulness. They drank more water that the crew of the plane provided; they laughed over apples and bananas, and milk and lemonade, and for the first time in months the smokers had cigarettes.

"But more than these was their kindness, their smiling friendliness," Ve'etutu said later.

Not one of the ten men had ever travelled in an aircraft before; everything was new, and especially the life-jackets, which they admired for their neatness. Not one of them felt nervous. When first they saw land through the aircraft window they prayed once more; they were in the habit of constant prayer, and it was still a consolation to them. Ve'etutu prayed this time.

The captain of the aircraft circled his machine while he told them to take a good look at the island where their captain had landed, the island of Kandavu. They were delighted to do so. But they were not as yet sure that it was their captain, for all that was known was that two men had landed and one had drowned. There was no indication of who it might be, and in their exhilaration of assured life they were also sad when they thought of their companion who had died.

The Buli Naceva, meanwhile, had set men from his eight villages to the task of searching the sea-verges for the body of Sateki; and before long they found the life-jacket that he had discarded. Not far away was the mystery that was David Fifita's chart, graved with the unidentified lines that had guided him to safety; they recognized that this was connected with the wreck and preserved it. A little while later they found *Malolelei*, empty of the possessions she had carried, the letters and the captain's log, the compass and sextant, and David's suitcase.

But they were amazed by the sweet construction of the little ship; they refused to believe, for a time, that it had been built without tools, until they looked closely at the butt-ends of the timbers, the char of the hot iron that had severed them, and the persistent mark of the spike.

The men from the reef were installed in the Colonial War Memorial Hospital in Suva, where doctors reported that none were seriously ill except for two they described as being "a bit dehydrated". These two, William Fa and

Finau Laione, had to be fed intravenously; and a later examination disclosed that Finau was suffering from tuberculosis, the germs of which he had either taken with him from Tonga or picked up from the Japanese wreck.

The aircraft had left South Minerva about 3.30 in the afternoon, and reached Suva shortly after dark. Its original intention, to return the men to Nuku'alofa, was frustrated by the lack of night-landing facilities there; and once they were in hospital it was some time before the men could be moved.

The hospital at Vunisea, meanwhile, had advised that it would be a week before David Fifita and David Uaisele were fit for sea travel. Uaisele in particular was very weak; his high consumption of liquid from the coconuts had endangered his life; but, rather than leave the men at Vunisea, the Commanding Officer from Lauthala sent the Sunderland to pick them up and return them to the company of their companions in the Suva hospital. A first attempt by the Sunderland to come in to Vunisea on Wednesday morning was abortive; they were prevented by rough seas; but in the afternoon it was brought in successfully and flew the two men back to Suva.

The tears still well into David's eyes when he talks of the kindness he encountered in Fiji. The people of Nacomotu village wept when they left, and when David made a little speech, thanking them for what they had done. The two men were given clothes to wear, and blankets, and a suitcase to carry what they could not put on. At Vunisea the police and the hospital staff made them other gifts, clothing and fruit and money.

But in their reunion with the others their happiness was tempered by the news of tragedy. David and Uaisele heard for the first time of the death of Fetaiaki Pulu; and for the first time they told how Sateki drowned. And Soakai, with the funeral of one son now arranged, heard from visitors of the death of Finau Lahi, his elder, though illegitimate, son who was killed in the boxing-ring in Nuku'alofa.

David was too ill to attend Fetaiaki's funeral arranged for the following Saturday; so were they all, except for Soakai and Ve'etutu. Fetaiaki was buried in the Nasinu cemetery after a service at the Centenary Methodist Church in Suva; and Tongan students from the Fiji School of Medicine were his pall-bearers.

There are many Tongans in Fiji, and all of them took the *Tuaikaepau* men to their hearts as heroes. By the Thursday of that week hospital authorities had to issue an official report:

A flood of kindness and admiration has swept over the survivors of the Tongan yacht *Tuaikaepau* since they were taken to the Colonial War Memorial Hospital on Tuesday. There have, however, been too many visitors for the good of the survivors. Now that the excitement of their rescue has died down, reaction is setting in among them, and they are all greatly in need of rest, which is an essential requirement for their quick recovery.

In view of this, and in the interests of the men, two of whom are so sick that they have to be fed intravenously, it is necessary that the flood of visitors, a majority of whom are Tongans, should be stemmed.

It has therefore been decided that normal visiting hours will have to be observed, and visits to the men outside these hours will not be allowed without special permission. The kindness, sympathy, and gifts from the public have been most welcome, but to assist the men's recovery they must be allowed periods of rest and relaxation.

The return of the men to their own country was scheduled for the afternoon of Monday, 22nd October; and one of the greatest of all feasts, in a country noted even in the hospitable Pacific for the lavishness of its feasts, had been prepared. The afternoon had been declared a public holiday, and from noon people had been streaming from distant villages as well as from Nuku'alofa to the harbour of Faa'ua, from which *Tuaikaepau* had sailed, and whither the men would return. By two o'clock the wharf and the mole surrounding the harbour were packed with people, and schoolchildren lined the mile-long road back into the town, right up to the entrance of the Government Malae and the Royal Palace beyond.

A little earlier, the close relatives of the survivors had been taken on board the *Kao*, the landing-craft which was to act as ferry from the flying-boat, so that they could welcome their men in privacy when the survivors arrived. The excitement was intense when the flying-boat touched down and taxied in; it was maintained while the *Kao* came slowly to the wharf; but when the first survivors stepped ashore there was a sudden hush that seemed to still the sounds of nature.

For they staggered rather than stepped; the weariness of all their trials was in their faces; they wore, designedly, the beards they had grown, except that David and Uaisele had shaved in Kandavu; and they looked stooped and old. David Fifita had lost 112 pounds of his weight; there were others who had lost seventy; but more than this it was their weariness, a certain quietude, that caused the hush.

The white-uniformed Police Band broke into the silence, playing the hymn, "Deep Harmony". The survivors, lining up, were greeted by the Deputy Premier of Tonga, Prince Tu'ipelehake, the second son of Queen Salote; for the Premier, her eldest son Tungi, was overseas. And His Royal Highness Tu'ipelehake, prepared as he was for the occasion, wearing the black of mourning and the old and worn mats that, in Tonga, complement this dress, had to wipe the tears from his eyes and compose himself before he spoke.

He thanked Squadron Leader O'Connor, who was present, for his rescue work; he thanked the doctors and the people and officials of Fiji. He commended the captain, the mate and the crew of *Tuaikaepau* for the way they had worked together and lived up to their Tongan traditions. He said that although it was with sadness he recalled that some had given their lives, it was with thankfulness he remembered that the majority had lived.

The survivors went on to an audience with Her Majesty Queen Salote, in the Royal Palace.

At the coronation of Elizabeth II of England in June 1953, Queen Salote won the hearts and the homage of all who saw her. She is a regal figure by any standards; her physical proportions are commanding; but it is even more obvious that, in her countenance, love and regality share equally. In her blood the pride of generations of forebears, revered through centuries that reach back to the dark mists of antiquity, has produced an anachronistic personality more suited than the imagination could conceive to the needs of the Tongan people for a leader in this age of change. She is an absolute monarch, under the protection of Great Britain; but she needs no such forms to bind her to the hearts of her people. If her word were not law, her wish would be; since her accession at the age of eighteen (in the year 1918) her every decision has been a wise one that increased her power and her popularity.

When Queen Salote attends, for example, one of the open-air concerts that are held from time to time on the Government Malae, the people who stud the lawns between the Queen and the ocean remain seated and quiet. Of their own volition they keep a respectful silence; they are overawed, in that small kingdom, by her presence.

The twelve survivors were driven from the harbour front to the palace office, there to make themselves ready for the audience the Queen would give them. Although from there it was only a few hundred yards to the palace, a white-painted two-storeyed building of New Zealand kauri (than which the world knows no better material), a special permission, unusual in Tonga, was given them to travel by bus to her door. This was necessary, for some of them could hardly stand.

On the palace verandah Queen Salote, Prince Tu'ipelehake, and attendants awaited them.

Led by David Fifita, the twelve survivors, each in his turn, knelt before Her Majesty to kiss, with reverence and with pride, the hand that she extended. When it came to the turn of Finau Laione he could go no further; he collapsed on his knees at her feet and remained there; and those who were privileged to see had tears in their eyes once again, each time her hand caressed his adolescent head. He had had his eighteenth birthday a day or two before in hospital in Fiji. He still looked young for his age.

The other survivors sat around, looking up at Her Majesty "like a group of children listening to their mother," as 'Uliti Palu, chief announcer for Tonga Radio, later described the scene. And Her Majesty addressed them quietly, like a mother talking to her children.

She told them that they had sailed away of their own free will on *Tuaikaepau*; they had been unfortunate enough to meet with disaster; but that in their subsequent predicament they had proved to the world they were capable of upholding the best Tongan traditions. They fully lived up to the Tongan motto that says, "The mountain of the Tongan is his heart."

They had also shown the world that when a Tongan was face to face with disaster or calamity the first thing he did was to turn to God. Even those who had not been to church for a long time had turned to God for protection. The Queen concluded by commending the captain in that he had given up his own son, so that he could accomplish his mission of obtaining help for his shipmates on the reef.

From their audience the survivors were driven to the Vaiola hospital, a mile or so away, and in the weeks of recovery they had time to assess, or to try to, the difference that the South Minerva Reef has made to their lives.

Finau, perhaps, was too young to put his thoughts into words, and perhaps he had been through too much of an ordeal. His tuberculosis has been arrested; he is putting on weight, for his great little heart, truly the mountain of this small Tongan, would not allow him to succumb easily.

His cousin Sipa Fine says he'd like to go to sea again; next time, though, in a vessel with a transmitter. He is going to write a book about his experiences; not for publication, just to show to his friends and some day, when he acquires one, his own family. He has a pound note that he had in his pocket; he proposes to stick this to one of the pages for an illustration. "But that's only if I don't have any desperate need of it before then," he qualified.

Fine Feuiaki thinks he will pay, in future, more attention to religion. He believes that the instrumentality of God was the only reason he survived. He feels that he was well led on the reef; Ve'etutu did a good job after David Fifita left. If there was another voyage going he would certainly want to go along.

Talo is still haunted by the deaths; but he can't see any reason why he too wouldn't sail again. William Fa says simply that on his first night home he couldn't sleep for happiness. The ordeal had a great effect on his personal life; and probably the greatest is that hereafter religion will take a more prominent part. He will take more interest in church affairs and try to earn prominence in that section of the community. And he will never forget the kindness and consideration of David Fifita.

Vaiangina Unga will never go on a small ship again; of that he's sure. He went to New Zealand as a sightseer only;

the motive was not sufficient to justify the ordeal it put him through. And he wouldn't choose, he thinks, to be under Fifita again if he were in a tight spot; but that is no reflection on the captain. It is simply that he doesn't think he'll get into that kind of tight spot again. He felt his faith deepened by his experience on the reef.

Soakai, for all his age, is thinking of getting into the ring again; and if the opportunity comes up he'll sail to New Zealand with David. As to religion, it was all right on the reef; but there was a little too much of it to bring back into a more normal existence.

David Uaisele is sure he'll go on the next voyage; he'll be sailing, he hopes, with David Fifita on *Taufale*, a ship much smaller than *Tuaikaepau*. He found a good friend on the reef in William Fa; they worked well together and came to a new kind of understanding. But in general, he thinks, the company he had on the reef could have been improved; one or two of the men, he says, were faint-hearted by his standards.

Saia Peni was never used to a seafaring life and now has no intention of becoming so. But he was not scared while he was on the reef. He didn't lose faith.

Teiapa'a Bloomfield is going to look for a wife. The wreck gave him his father back; he feels that it has steadied his life; and while he was happy, and rather proud, to have had a whole crowd of girl-friends in the past, now he thinks he'd like to get married and raise a family. He hasn't as yet any particular girl in mind; instead he has a particular way of life.

It was a good crowd, he says, to be shipwrecked with. He admired the way his old friend Soakai piled in, ripping timber off the wreck to build the *Malolelei*, and diving deeper than anyone else to recover the cane-knife. But he made a new friend, and a new kind of friend for him, in the sober Vaiangina.

David Fifita sat up on his hospital bed and thought it over. Alapasita was near by, looking far younger than her years, her face unlined, though she has had more than the normal worries of a wife with her man at sea. She did not look like the mother of eight children, but some of her nearly grown daughters were at hand, in neat school uniforms, bringing tea and cakes to their father and his guests.

David said, "When it happens again that I am lost on a reef, all I want is that it should be the same crowd with me. I don't mean I want to be lost on another reef—no, no; never that—but if I am I will be happy to have the same men with me. I had no trouble with them at all; they all worked together and did what they could. There were times when they were a bit unhappy; when we were first there we thought we would be looked for and rescued, and when we weren't, that was disappointing for them. And certainly they stole the water from time to time, but there was a great deal of pressure on them to do that. And at times those that stole would go without to give a little more to the sick; the stealing was not as bad as it might sound. There was the disappointment day after day, but then I thought, when they were all settled down we would build a boat. And that is what we did."

As soon as he could get about David paid a ceremonial visit to Tofa Ramsay, who had owned the *Tuaikaepau*, which carried no insurance. Tofa had met him at the wharf on the return from Fiji; on that occasion they shook hands and that was all. But the first Sunday that David was better he called on Tofa. He said:

"I've come to give you a chance to abuse me, to be angry with me, and to have your say in anger because I lost your ship. To give you a chance to let out your anger, and to let out your sadness too by talking to me. I want you to know that it was through no stupidity, nor was it

198

through any neglect, nor was it through any fault of mine that we were wrecked. I did what I could.

"To my dying day," David continued, "I will never forget the wreck, and I will do all in my power to help you, and perhaps to enable you to replace this ship with another." He dwelt upon the sadness he felt at the loss of a fine ship. Then he continued:

"I am a man of the sea. It is no good for me to turn to the land. I am like a man with a bad wound on his hand. I have been to the doctor and had him look to it, bathe it and salve it and bandage it. In time the wound will heal, but it will leave a scar. I will carry the scar that is the loss of *Tuaikaepau* to my dying day, nor will I ever be able to overlook or to forget it, until somehow I have helped to replace your ship.

"Perhaps I can get to a bigger country, and work and use my hands there, to earn the money for another boat.

"If I remain in Tonga I will die an old man, because I am useless here; I haven't any earning capacity except at sea or abroad. Perhaps I could take a team of lads on the *Taufale* to New Zealand or to Sydney, and we could all get work at Westfield, at a freezing works or some such place, and by living on the boat save money to replace the *Tuaikaepau*."

Tofa regarded this as a kind and generous offer. He told David, well, concentrate on getting your health back and we will talk about it. He was sympathetic to David, though he feels, as he told some associates, that he wouldn't have lost the *Tuaikaepau* had he been aboard. He would have known that there was a chance of reef being in the vicinity; and, that being so, would not have left the deck. He would have been very alert. Tofa trusts his captains, but in addition to trusting them he constantly checks up on them whenever he is aboard.

Nevertheless his admiration for David's navigational

ability is still high; and the magnificent job that David did on the reef will, he knows, establish David's reputation for all time as a leader of men.

Back in the hospital, David waited for the days to pass and his strength to return. A reporter one day commented on the fact that throughout the entire voyage he had had no luck running his way, except for the presence of the Japanese wreck upon the reef. But David was not sure that that had been lucky.

When he was asked, "But what would you have done had there been no wreck to shelter you?" he replied instantly, "We'd have been back in Tonga in two weeks, the lot of us."

The reporter was incredulous, but David was serious, and apparently regretted that they had not moved on their own initiative from the beginning.

"Well, we had the raft there; we'd built it that night. And the wind was with us, blowing straight to Tonga. We'd either have got back in two weeks or we'd all have perished. But we would have done something." It was obvious that he did not seriously entertain the thought of failure.

Another reporter, John Carter from the *Fiji Times*, had a question for him.

"The sea has taken your father and your son. Do you think the sea is cruel?"

David Fifita thought about that only a second, and shook his head.

"I don't think the sea is cruel. I love the sea very much, and I'll go back to it. There is no cruelty in the sea. It moves as God wants it to move. I fight it, and I never give up. That is why I fought it on the reef, and again near the island of Kandavu. I never give way to the sea. I love it. But I don't know why."

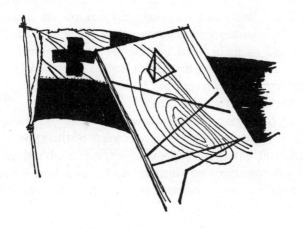

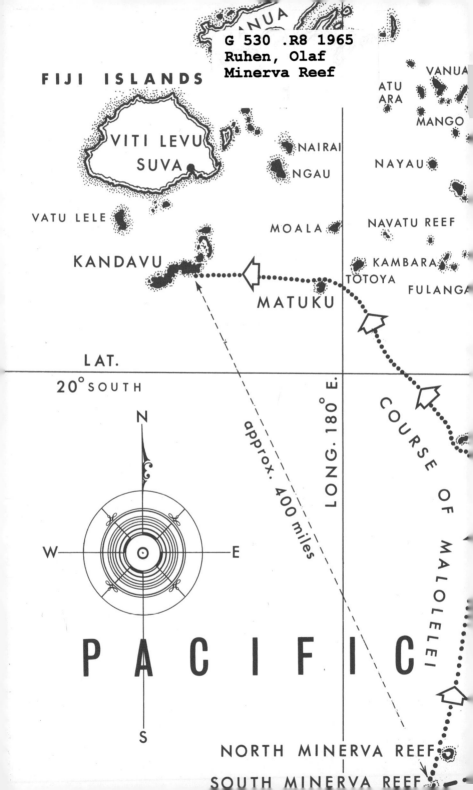

FIJI ISLANDS

VANUA

VITI LEVU
SUVA

VATU LELE

KANDAVU

MATUKU

NAIRAI

NGAU

MOALA

ATU
ARA

MANGO

NAYAU

NAVATU REEF

KAMBARA

TOTOYA

FULANGA

VANUA

LAT.

20° SOUTH

N

W   E

S

approx. 400 miles

LONG. 180° E.

COURSE OF MALOLELEI

PACIFIC

NORTH MINERVA REEF

SOUTH MINERVA REEF